search Institute

he Status
of Gender
Integration in
the Military

Analysis of
Selected Occupations

Margaret C. Harrell ✦ **Megan K. Beckett**

Chiaying Sandy Chien ✦ **Jerry M. Sollinger**

RAND

Prepared for the
Office of the Secretary of Defense

The research described in this report was sponsored by the Office of the Secretary of Defense (OSD). The research was conducted in RAND's National Defense Research Institute, a federally funded research and development center supported by the OSD, the Joint Staff, the unified commands, and the defense agencies under Contract DASW01-01-C-0004.

Library of Congress Cataloging-in-Publication Data

The status of gender integration in the military : analysis of selected occupations /
    Margaret C. Harrell ... [et al.].
        p. cm.
    "MR-1380."
    Includes bibliographical references.
    ISBN 0-8330-3093-0
        1. United States—Armed Forces—Women. 2. United States—Armed Forces—
    Occupational specialties. 3. United States—Armed Forces—Personnel manage
    ment. I. Harrell, Margaret C.

    UB418.W65 S735 2002
    358.4'0082—dc21

                                                                    2002021397

RAND is a nonprofit institution that helps improve policy and decisionmaking through research and analysis. RAND® is a registered trademark. RAND's publications do not necessarily reflect the opinions or policies of its research sponsors.

Published 2002 by RAND
1700 Main Street, P.O. Box 2138, Santa Monica, CA 90407-2138
1200 South Hayes Street, Arlington, VA 22202-5050
201 North Craig Street, Suite 202, Pittsburgh, PA 15213-1516
RAND URL: http://www.rand.org/
To order RAND documents or to obtain additional information,
contact Distribution Services: Telephone: (310) 451-7002;
Fax: (310) 451-6915; Email: order@rand.org

RAND's National Defense Research Institute (NDRI) was asked to assess the degree to which women are represented in the military occupations open to them and to determine whether there are factors that inappropriately hinder or preclude women's opportunities to work within their military specialties. Specifically, this work addresses whether women and men are receiving equal opportunities to work in selected occupations. Second, this analysis considers whether the number of women who can enter the selected occupations is limited, despite the occupation being open to women. This research included statistical analysis of all military occupations and detailed analysis of selected occupations. The statistical analysis is summarized herein but is published in more detail in a companion volume (Beckett and Chien, 2002).

This study was sponsored by the Under Secretary of Defense for Personnel and Readiness and was carried out in the Forces and Resources Policy Center of RAND's National Defense Research Institute, a federally funded research and development center sponsored by the Office of the Secretary of Defense, the Joint Staff, and the defense agencies. This work should be of interest to military service members, military policymakers, Congress, any media interested in the status of gender integration in the U.S. military, and academics and researchers interested in gender and work or gender and organizations.

CONTENTS

BACKGROUND

The early history of women in the military services was largely one of restriction, with stringent limits on where they could serve, what they could do, and what units they could join. Beginning in 1992, marked changes in law and policy have dramatically altered this situation. First, Congress repealed the combat exclusion laws, making it possible for women to fly combat aircraft and serve on combat vessels. Second, the Department of Defense (DoD) replaced the risk rule, which restricted women from assignments based on the "risk of exposure to direct combat, hostile fire, or capture" with a restriction on direct ground combat. The latter restriction was based on the probability of any given occupation or assignment leading to involvement in direct ground combat. These changes had two effects: new skills—and new units—opened to women.

DoD previously asked NDRI to study the effects of these expanded opportunities for women on the readiness, cohesion, and morale of the forces. The results of that study showed negligible effects on these aspects of the military services but also showed that the progress of integrating women into the new occupations was slow (Harrell and Miller, 1997).

Subsequent to the NDRI study, the U.S. General Accounting Office (GAO) published two reports that raised some issues related to gender (GAO, 1998, 1999). More specifically, the reports questioned whether service requirements were being used to exclude women from occupations that were open to them and whether women and men were getting equal opportunities to work in their specialties.

The reports also noted that, while women were moving into untraditional occupations, the closure of some units to them limited the number of women who could enter an occupation. Finally, GAO noted that, because they lacked exposure to certain subject areas, women were scoring low on certain segments of the aptitude test the military uses.

THIS REPORT

Partly in response to the GAO reports and partly to follow up on the earlier study, DoD asked NDRI to examine the extent of gender integration of positions opened to women as a result of the legislative and policy changes of the early 1990s. Specifically, the department wanted to determine whether men and women were getting equal opportunities to work in selected occupations and whether there were barriers that barred women from an occupation even though it was formally open to them.[1]

To answer these questions, our research involved two steps. First, we did a broad statistical analysis of female representation in occupations newly opened to women, that is, since the legislative and policy changes. Second, we did a more focused analysis of specific occupations, examining ten in some detail. We sought a cross section of occupations by service, rank, nature of the work, level of gender representation in the occupation, and level of representation in the occupational class (group of occupations). Table S.1 includes the occupations selected for a more detailed analysis and summarizes some of that research.

This table indicates that the occupations selected for case study analysis can be divided into three categories based upon the level of female representation evident in each. The "most progress" category includes one Army, one Marine Corps, and two Navy occupations.

---

[1]In this book, we make the following distinctions between terms: An individual's *occupation* or *career* is the field in which he or she received training (e.g., cook or infantryman). The *billet* or *position* refers to the need for such individuals within a given unit. For example, there may be billets for four cooks on a particular ship or several hundred infantrymen in an unit. The *unit* refers to the organization to which that individual is assigned, such as a particular ship or battalion.

Table S.1

Summary of Occupations Examined

Occupation	Nature of Work	Female[a]		Occupational Class	% Female Increasing ?	Accessions Compared to Service Overall	Training Completion Rates Compared to Males	Assignment or Career Restrictions
		No.	%					
Little Progress Toward Gender Integration								
Air Force F-16 Pilot (Officer)	Fighter aviation High tech.	21	1.30	Tactical Operations	Yes	N/A: Pilots	Comparable	None
USMC F/A-18 Pilot (Officer)	Fighter aviation High tech.	1	0.25	Tactical Operations	No	N/A: Pilots	N/A—numbers too small	One nonflying assignment closed No career impact
USMC Combat Engineer (1371) (Enlisted)	Heavy, dirty Field conditions	34	1.30	Infantry, Gun Crews, and Seamanship	No	Lower	Comparable or better	Yes—46% closed Career impact

Table S.1—Continued

Occupation	Nature of Work	Female[a] No.	Female[a] %	Occupational Class	% Female Increasing ?	Accessions Compared to Service Overall	Training Completion Rates Compared to Males	Assignment or Career Restrictions
Some Progress Toward Gender Integration								
Army AH-64 Apache Aviator (152F/H) (Warrant Officer)	Helicopter aviation High tech.	14	1.36	Tactical Operations	Yes	N/A: Pilots	Comparable	None
Army Field Artillery Surveyor (82C) (Enlisted)	Dirty Field conditions	52	7.00	Other Technical and Allied Specialist	No	Lower	Comparable	Yes—70% closed Career impact, job being phased out
Navy Gunner's Mate (Enlisted)	Diverse conditions Extensive sea duty	183	4.35	Infantry, Gun Crews, and Seamanship	Yes, slowly	Lower	Comparable	Yes, smaller ships No career impact

Table S.1—Continued

Occupation	Nature of Work	Female[a] No.	%	Occupational Class	% Female Increasing?	Accessions Compared to Service Overall	Training Completion Rates Compared to Males	Assignment or Career Restrictions
Most Progress Toward Gender Integration								
Army Bridge Crewmember (12C) (Enlisted)	Heavy, dirty Field conditions	148	16.53	Infantry, Gun Crews, and Seamanship	Yes	Higher	Lower	None
USMC Air Support (7242) (Enlisted)	Field conditions	27	11.00	Communications and Intelligence Specialists	No	Comparable	Comparable	None currently applied
Navy Sonar Technician-Surface (Enlisted)	High tech Extensive sea duty	389	10.13	Electronic Equipment Repairers	Yes	Comparable	Slightly lower	Yes, smaller ships No career impact
Navy Surface Warfare Officer (Officer)	Extensive sea duty	914	11.30	Tactical Operations	Yes	Higher	Comparable	Very few, very small ships No career impact

aData as of 2001.

They include both officer and enlisted occupations, a range of environments, and both demanding physical labor and highly technical work. These differences underscore the extent to which gender analysis should consider occupations on an individual basis.

COMPLICATING FACTORS

Several factors complicated our analysis, and these should be kept in mind when reviewing our results. Some of these are specific to a service, and others cut across all services. One service-specific item pertains to the Navy: the process of modifying ships to accommodate women. In some cases, providing separate berthing and sanitary facilities for women on ships can slow the rate of integration, even if a particular skill group is open. Second, service obligations can make it difficult to identify retention trends. For example, going to flight school carries with it a substantial service obligation. The long obligation can mask a retention problem, and it will take some time to determine retention trends accurately. Another issue is that some of the decision processes that affect occupational choices are opaque. For example, the determination of aircraft-specific follow-on training involves student preference, instructor recommendation, and performance in basic flight school. Thus, it may not be clear whether student enrollment for a specific type of flight training results from student choice, performance in basic flight training, or perhaps institutional biases. Finally, relatively few women are involved in many of the occupations, and the retention or resignation of a single individual can skew the results significantly. In addition, it is not clear that the first women in a newly opened occupation will encounter the same experiences or behave similarly to their successors.

For these reasons, we present our statistical analysis primarily as a benchmark for future work. The case study analysis is limited by design but presents some insightful patterns regarding gender integration.

WHAT WE FOUND OUT

Our more-detailed analysis of the ten occupations lead us to a number of conclusions:

Success at achieving gender representation is mixed. Of the ten occupations studied, female representation is increasing in half. For example, in the Army, women are overrepresented in the Bridge Crewmember occupation, and their numbers are increasing. However, they are underrepresented in the artillery surveyor skill, and their numbers are declining. In the Marine Corps, numbers are falling among field engineers. The numbers are not increasing in the air support occupation, but the percentage of women in the skill exceeds that of women in the Marine Corps. Female representation is increasing among Air Force F-16 pilots but not among Marine Corps F/A-18 pilots.

Such metrics as the level of female representation and the percentage of accessions that are female are useful as benchmarks but need to be understood in the context of an individual occupation. There are valid reasons, such as the length of the average career and the time the occupation will take to become fully integrated, that some occupations have less female representation. In these cases, the statistical evaluations are useful as benchmarks for further analysis but cannot be used in a single snapshot to indicate "significant" levels of representation or underrepresentation. Additionally, the rate at which female representation is increasing may also be misleading if the occupation is integrated at an appropriate level (and definitions of "appropriate level" vary), if the occupation is being terminated to all personnel, if the occupation is being closed to women, or if increasing representation in a particular occupation is a result of limited opportunities in other occupations.

Nature of the work does not alone affect gender representation. The nature of the work involved in the occupations does not seem to affect the willingness of women to enter it. Neither the hard physical work of the engineering occupations nor the austere living conditions of the air support skill appear to deter women from seeking to work in the jobs. Additionally, high-technology occupations that operate in relatively more comfortable circumstances do not necessarily draw women in greater numbers. Navy sonar technicians work with sophisticated electronic equipment in relatively comfortable surroundings. This occupation has lower female representation than does the Navy overall.

Accession models and processes may require adjustment. The services determine how many women they want to recruit into a specific occupation by using different accession models. Some of the data developed in this study suggest that the models may need to be adjusted. For example, the Marine Corps has decided to stop recruiting women for the Field Engineer occupation, but the current female representation in that skill is only 1.3 percent compared with 6 percent overall in the enlisted ranks. Additionally, the Armed Services Vocational Aptitude Battery (ASVAB) tests, which are prerequisites for these occupations, are biased toward test takers with prior exposure to the subjects. This bias disadvantages women. Among the occupations examined herein, the ASVAB test requirements did not preclude the services from meeting the female accession targets. However, this could currently be a barrier in other occupations or in these occupations in the future.

Women do about as well as men in training. The data show that women do about as well as men in the skill training or only slightly worse. The small numbers involved make this a difficult area for analysis, but nothing in this research suggests that women will have difficulty performing well in nontraditional occupations.

Some skills have assignment limitations that make it unlikely for a woman to have a viable career. Assignment constraints can pose a problem for integration. For example, 70 percent of assignments for Army Field Artillery Surveyors and almost half of assignments for Marine Corps Combat Engineers are closed to women. However, the services have different models and methods for translating these assignment limitations into targeted levels of female representation.

Predicting future levels of gender integration is difficult. Several issues make it difficult to predict future levels of integration. First, if the women do not enter directly into a skill and must first undergo a long period of training, as they must to become a pilot, it is difficult to tease out the factors affecting integration. Second, the small numbers involved in many of the skills complicate making future estimates. Service obligations further complicate the problem. Finally, the first women in a field frequently experience a "pioneer effect." As a result, neither their experiences nor their performance in the occupation may be the same as those of their successors. As the first representatives of their gender in a field, these women may feel extra pressure to succeed. Thus, early completion and retention rates may not be typical. It will not be until some years have passed and the presence of women is regarded as routine that it will be possible to identify representative trends.

RECOMMENDATIONS AND POLICY IMPLICATIONS

Do not let women join occupations that are going to merge with ones closed to women. The issue for the services is more than ensuring a representative number of women in a given occupation. It is also ensuring that the skill fields offered to women can provide them a viable career. Thus, women should not be encouraged to enter skill areas that a service plans to merge with others that are not open to women. Furthermore, the service needs to develop a plan for how to deal with the women in the occupation when it does merge with another.

Verify and validate the service models that limit female accessions as a result of assignments closed to women. All services need to review the models that determine the targeted number for female accessions to ensure that the assumptions and inputs are not inappropriately limiting female accessions.

Ensure that publicly available information, such as that on official recruiting Web sites, provides accurate information about opportunities available to women.

Account for the pioneer effect. The services should recognize that the initial trends of women entering new occupations may not be representative of what will occur later.

Recognize that female representation needs to be understood by occupation.

Do not assume that female service members will lack interest in jobs with seemingly less-appealing work environments.

Counsel incoming personnel about the career opportunities available to them in various occupations. If no advancement opportunities are available within a given occupation, the incoming recruit should be informed. Lack of opportunities for promotion may dissuade a new recruit from selecting that occupation. However, if the skills to be gained translate well to civilian occupations (as is the case, for example, for Marine Corps Combat Engineers), limited

opportunities within the military occupation may not deter accessions. While this is more likely to be an issue for women entering
occupations with limited assignment opportunities for women (and
thus limited advancement opportunities), both male and female
recruits should fully understand the career opportunities available to
them.

**Promote analysis of trends in accession, training, assignment, and
retention data by gender.** "Gender-blind" data records serve little
purpose other than to simplify the daily activities of those who maintain the records. Such records obscure both negative and positive
trends. As a result, the services recognize neither when they need to
address problems nor when they can applaud successful integration
and capitalize on positive trends.

**Conduct further research into the role of individual experiences
and decisionmaking processes in occupation selection, assignment
selection, and retention.**

**Conduct further research to understand the role of individual deci-
sionmaking in aircraft selection.** Such research should illuminate
the reasons quality flight students, both male and female, are
neglecting to fly jet aircraft.

ACKNOWLEDGMENTS

We are grateful for assistance from Col Sheila Earle, U.S. Air Force; Bradford Loo; and CDR Leslie Quinn, U.S. Navy, of our sponsoring office. Additionally, LTC Margaret Flott, U.S. Army; LTJG Summer Jones and CAPT Sarah McCullom, U.S. Navy; Capt Emi Izawa, U.S. Air Force; and LtCol. Craig Timberlake, Maj. Andrew Gilmore, and Capt. Antonio Martinez, U.S. Marine Corps, were invaluable in their roles as primary service contacts as we conducted this research.

This work depended heavily upon the cooperation of many offices throughout the services as we gained an understanding of the current status of gender integration and of how the selected occupations were managed. Thus, we appreciate the assistance of the following individuals, who all willingly contributed their time and assistance. We list them below by service, in alphabetical order:

Army: CW5 Mike Adair, Steve Bell, CW3 George Ciminale, MAJ Coakley, CW4 Robert Cox, SFC Woodrow Jones, SFC Richard S. Law, LTC John R. Luce, Douglas McCann, SGM John Rather, LTC William A. Rigby, MAJ Burton Shields, LTC Paul D. Thornton, LTC Stephen K. Walker, and CW4 Johnny Warren.

Navy: CDR David Caldwell, STGCS Patrick Gustafson, LTC Rebecca Harper, CAPT Joseph Harriss, LT Matt Hawks, CDR Jim Hooper, LCDR Stephen Kozloski, STGCS Eric William Page, CDR John Peterson, STGC Robert Polk, FCCM(SW) Kirk Snyder, and GMC(SW) William J. Yeo.

Air Force: Col Bill Faucher, Lt Col Scott Frost, Lt Col Gregory Hayman, and Cathi Labonte.

Marine Corps: Maj. John W. Bicknell, Maj. Freddie J. Blish, Maj. Sean C. Blochberger, GySgt Larry B. Brinson, Maj. Rod D. Burnett, Maj. Timothy Foster, Col. William L. Groves, Capt. Thomas H. Koloski, LtCol. Mark D. McMannis, Maj. David L. Ross, GySgt Reginald Smith, and Maj. Philip Zimmerman.

This work was improved by the careful reviews of Harry Thie (RAND), Laura Miller (Department of Sociology, University of California at Los Angeles), and Carol Cohn (Department of Sociology and Anthropology, Bowdoin College). We also appreciate the assistance of Audrey Caudle, Iris Sanchez, and Robin Cole during this research.

ABBREVIATIONS

AFAST	Alternative Flight Aptitude Selection Test
AGF	auxiliary command ship
AIT	Advanced Individual Training
AOE	fast combat support ship
AOR	replenishment oiler
API	Aviation Preflight Indoctrination
ARS	rescue and salvage ship
AS	Auto and Shop Information (score)
AS	submarine tender
ASVAB	Armed Services Vocational Aptitude Battery
AW	Aviation Warfare Systems Operator
CG	cruiser
CMF	Career Management Field (Army)
CONUS	continental United States
CV	aircraft carrier
CVN	aircraft carrier, nuclear
DD	destroyer
DDG	guided missile destroyer
DMDC	Defense Manpower Data Center

DoD	Department of Defense
EAS	end of active service
EOD	Explosive Ordnance Disposal
EWO	Electronic Warfare Officer
FAC	forward air controller
FAST	Flight Aptitude Selection Test
FF	frigate
FFG	guided missile frigate
FY	fiscal year
GAO	U.S. General Accounting Office
GD	General Science (score?)
GM	Gunner's Mate (used for pay grade E-7 and above)
GMG	Gunner's Mate-Guns
GMM	Gunner's Mate-Missiles
LCC	amphibious command ship
LHA	amphibious warfare ship
LHD	amphibious warfare ship
LPD	amphibious warfare ship
LSD	amphibious warfare ship
LST	amphibious warfare ship
MAW	Marine air wing
MCM	mine countermeasures ship
MCS	mine countermeasure command and control ship
MEU	Marine Expeditionary Unit
MHC	coastal mine hunter
MOS	Military Occupational Specialty
NATO	North Atlantic Treaty Organization

NCO	noncommissioned officer
NDRI	National Defense Research Institute
NEC	Navy Enlisted Classification
OCONUS	outside the continental United States
OPMD	Officer Personnel Management Directorate
OSUT	One Station Unit Training
PADS	Positional Azimuth Determining System
PC	patrol coastal ship
PERSCOM	Army Personnel Command
Perstempo	Personnel tempo
ROTC	Reserve Officer Training Corps
SEALs	Sea, Air, Land (special warfare unit)
SSBN	submarine, nuclear
SSN	submarine
STG	Sonar Technician-Surface
STG	Sonar Technician-Advanced Electronics Field
SUPT	Specialized Undergraduate Pilot Training
SWO	Surface Warfare Officer
TBS	The Basic School (initial training for Marine Corps officers)
UIC	Unit Identification Code
USMC	U.S. Marine Corps
VLS	Vertical Launch System
VMA	Table 2.6
VMAW	Undefined
VMFA	Undefined
WAAC	Women's Army Auxiliary Corps

| WAVES | Women Accepted for Volunteer Emergency Service |
| WSO | Weapon System Officer |

Chapter One

INTRODUCTION

BACKGROUND[1]

The roles women can play in the military have been limited ever since the services started accepting them. About 33,000 women served in World War I—20,000 of them in the Army and Navy Nurse Corps, which were separate from the regular Army and Navy. In World War II, manpower shortages and reports of valuable performance by women in other countries' armed forces led the United States to use approximately 350,000 women for its own military effort. The attack on Pearl Harbor resulted in the creation of the Women's Army Auxiliary Corps (WAAC) and Women Accepted for Volunteer Emergency Service (WAVES). Women typically filled nursing and administrative jobs, which were consistent with civilian women's work, although they also served in all other noncombat jobs. These 350,000 women who served in World War II were regarded as temporary support that would free more men for combat.

After the war, women's future role with the military was called into question. In 1948, the year when racial integration was mandated by President Harry S. Truman, Congress passed the Women's Armed Services Integration Act, which placed highly specific limits on the women who would now be allowed to join the Army. Women could make up no more than 2 percent of the total enlisted ranks; the proportion of female officers could equal no more than 10 percent of enlisted women. No woman could serve in a command position,

---

[1]This background material was drawn from Harrell and Miller (1997).

attain the rank of general, or hold permanent rank above lieutenant colonel. This act specifically prohibited women from being assigned to aircraft or ships engaged in combat missions. Because the Navy and the Air Force have the most ships and aircraft, this act applied most directly to them. However, the Secretary of the Army developed policies to exclude women from direct combat, based upon the implied congressional intent of the Navy and Air Force statutes.[2]

The doors for women have been pried open slowly over the past four decades. In 1967, the 2-percent cap on enlisted women and some promotion restrictions were lifted; in 1972, the Reserve Officer Training Corps (ROTC) was opened to women; in 1976, the first women entered the service academies; in 1978, Navy women were assigned to noncombatant ships and the Women's Army Corps was dissolved; in 1989, two women commanded units in Panama; in 1990, the first female commanded a Navy ship; and in 1991, in the Persian Gulf War, large numbers of women moved forward with their units into combat zones, which they were officially forbidden to enter. In 1988, a Department of Defense (DoD) Task Force on Women in the Military created the "risk rule" to bar women from areas on the battlefield where the "risk of exposure to direct combat, hostile fire, or capture is equal to or greater than that experienced by associated combat units in the same theater of operations." This rule proved very problematic and difficult to interpret.

The years 1992 through 1994 saw considerable legislative and policy changes regarding the roles of women in the military. The National Defense Authorization Acts for FYs 1992 and 1993 repealed the combat exclusion law that had prohibited women from being permanently assigned to combat aircraft. In April 1993, Les Aspin, then Secretary of Defense, sent a memorandum to the services that stated

> Two years ago, Congress repealed the law that prohibited women from being assigned to combat aircraft. It is now time to implement that mandate and address the remaining restrictions on the assignment of women. (Aspin, 1993.)

This memorandum directed the services to give women the opportunity to compete for assignment to combat aircraft and to open as

---

[2]For a detailed history of women in the military, see Holm (1982).

many Navy ships to women as possible under the legal restrictions that still prevented them from being assigned to ships engaged in combat missions. The memorandum also directed the Army and the Marine Corps to study further opportunities for women but did not prescribe additional gender integration in these two services. Instead, it reaffirmed the exclusion of women from units below the brigade level whose primary mission entailed direct combat on the ground.

Two critical changes in law and policy pertaining to the assignment of service women were implemented in FY 1994. First, the National Defense Authorization Act for FY 1994 repealed the legal restrictions that had prohibited women from being assigned to combatant vessels. This act also established important guidelines for the integration of women into previously closed occupations when it also required the Secretary of Defense to

- Ensure that qualification for and continuance in occupational career fields is evaluated on the basis of a common, relevant performance standard and not on the basis of gender;
- Refrain from the use of gender quotas, goals, or ceilings, except as specifically authorized by Congress; and
- Refrain from changing occupational standards simply to increase or decrease the number of women in an occupational career field.[3]

Second, the Secretary of Defense rescinded the risk rule in January 1994 (Aspin, 1994). Instead of closing noncombatant positions or units based upon the risk to personnel in those units, this memorandum directed that women be assigned to all units except those "below the brigade level whose primary mission is to engage in direct combat on the ground." *Direct ground combat* was defined as

engaging an enemy on the ground with individual or crew served weapons, while being exposed to hostile fire and to a high probability of direct physical contact with the hostile force's personnel. Direct ground combat takes place well forward on the battlefield

---

[3]Quoted from U.S. House of Representatives, undated.

> while locating and closing with the enemy to defeat them by fire, maneuver, or shock effect. (Aspin, 1994.)

The memorandum also directed that this guidance would be used only to expand opportunities to women and not to close units or positions that had previously been open to them.

Two kinds of opportunities resulted from the1992–1994 legislative and policy changes. First, new occupations, or skills, opened to women. Second, units that had previously been closed to women because of the risk rules now opened to women.

Given these changes, the House Report for the National Defense Authorization Act for Fiscal Year 1997 directed the Secretary of Defense

> to obtain an independent study by an FFRDC [federally funded research and development center] evaluating the performance of each military service in integrating women into military occupations previously closed. As part of this study, the FFRDC shall evaluate the effect on defense readiness and morale of integrating women in newly opened occupations and positions as well as factors affecting the pace at which military services are integrating women.

The Office of the Secretary of Defense asked RAND to undertake this study (see Harrell and Miller, 1997). In addition to addressing issues of readiness, cohesion, and morale related to gender integration, this prior RAND study confirmed that, in response to the policy and legislative changes, the services had opened more occupations and organizations to women. Table 1.1 shows the change in the number of positions, or billets, opened to women as a result of these changes in the occupations and units open to women.

Clearly, progress had occurred in all services. However, the study determined that the numbers of women in some newly opened occupations and positions were still disproportionately low.

There were several valid reasons for such underrepresentation, such as the training pipelines that feed the newly opened Air Force pilot and navigator positions. Some newly opened occupations lacked any female volunteers (although it is unclear the extent to which recruiters were encouraging young women to enter nontraditional

Table 1.1

**Positions Opened to Women Before and
After Legislative and Policy Changes**

| | Positions Open (%) | |
| | Before | After Law, |
Service	April 1993	Policy Changes
Army	61.0	67.2
Navy	61.0	94.0
Air Force	97.0	99.7
Marine Corps	33.0	62.0
DoD Total	67.4	80.2

NOTE: While 94 percent of all Navy positions are available to women, only approximately 13 percent of all shipboard bunks will be female berthing at the end of the current embarkation plan. Thus, the percentage of Navy positions that could be simultaneously filled with women is less than 94 percent.

occupations), and many young women did not score well enough on the prerequisite tests to be eligible for the newly opened technical occupations.

In some cases, the occupation or skill was open to women, but not all the positions coded with that occupation were open to women because, within that occupation, the women could only be assigned at certain organizational levels, e.g., brigade or higher. While this policy is valid within the guidelines established, the effects of these limitations on both men and women in the career field are uncertain. The study also asserted that invalid limitations also exist and that the limits operate in complex ways. Some positions that are technically open to women may actually be closed because the position is coded to be filled by a skill closed to women, e.g., drill sergeant positions coded with an infantry Military Occupational Specialty (MOS). While some such positions may be appropriately coded, there is no method, other than to check each position individually, to determine whether the MOS coding is valid. Finally, the research found some informal limitations, such as the commander who will not have a driver or an aide of the opposite sex due to the concern of rumors or potential charges of sexual harassment. In other cases, a commander had a woman assigned to an untraditional position, but she actually performed duty in another.

Following the publication of the 1997 RAND study, a General Accounting Office (GAO) report recommended that the Secretary of Defense direct the services to assess (1) whether requirements for skills or specialties that are presently closed to women are being used inappropriately as prerequisites for positions that are otherwise open to women and (2) whether men or women are receiving an equal opportunity to work within the area of their military specialty (GAO, 1998). The department concurred with this recommendation and agreed to assess the issues. An initial assessment that the Office of the Secretary of Defense and the services conducted concluded that, to obtain a thorough and fair assessment, an outside study should be conducted. A second GAO report addressed the occupational distribution of military women (GAO, 1999). Among other things, GAO found that, although military women continue to work primarily in health care, administration, personnel, and supply occupations, they are beginning to enter more nontraditional fields. However, the report pointed to two institutional barriers to gender integration in the military. First, because some units are closed to women, the number of women who can enter career fields that occur in closed units is limited, even though that occupation is open to women. Second, women tend not to score well on certain portions of the Armed Services Vocational Aptitude Battery (ASVAB) test because they measure prior knowledge in, rather than aptitude for, certain subjects, such as machine shop and electronics repair.

SCOPE AND METHODOLOGY OF THIS RESEARCH EFFORT

It was in the context of these GAO reports that the Office of Officer and Enlisted Personnel Management, organized under the Assistant Secretary of Defense (Force Management Policy), sponsored this effort to address the gender integration of positions newly opened to women and the paths that lead to these positions. This analysis is intended to address two of the issues highlighted in the GAO reports. First, we examine whether women and men are receiving equal opportunities to work in selected occupations. Second, we consider whether the number of women who can enter the selected occupations is limited, despite the occupation being open to women.

To address these two issues, we set two tasks for ourselves. The first was a broad statistical analysis to determine how many women are assigned to the positions that are open to them. It emphasized the occupations that opened as a result of the legislative and policy changes of the early 1990s. This analysis updated our data about how women are distributed among the newly opened occupations. It also identified the occupations that have low female representation, compared to the representation in the appropriate military service. This analysis took into account the time that has elapsed since integration began; this is an important consideration in any assessment of diversity in a closed system because it will take time for women to progress through these careers. Thus, this statistical analysis provides a benchmark for future comparisons.

This first task provides statistical support for a consideration of equal opportunity, or whether women have the same options available to them regarding entry into and success in military careers within the military. A lack of such equal opportunities for women indicates the presence of barriers. Some barriers, such as those that limit the numbers of women in seagoing occupations due to berthing considerations on ships, are likely legitimate. Other barriers, which do not have a credible justification, are not legitimate.

Because an assessment of the existence and legitimacy of any barriers requires a qualitative approach, the second task of this research builds on the first. It takes the quantitative output and focuses on selected career fields to determine whether the level of representation most likely results from time elapsed, systemic barriers, or individual choice.

INTENT AND ORGANIZATION OF THIS REPORT

The text below describes the methodology and data sources we used in this study. Chapter Two summarizes our data analysis across the services, including the number of occupations and positions closed to women, as well as the level of gender representation in previously and newly opened occupations and units. Chapter Three provides more-detailed analysis for selected occupations. Chapter Four presents observations and conclusions. A companion volume (Beckett and Chien, 2002) provides detailed information on the distribution of women across occupations and units available in the data.

DATA AND METHODOLOGY

Phase One

To examine the representation of women across occupations and units in each of the services, we use data from the Defense Manpower Data Center's (DMDC's) March 1998 Personnel Tempo (Perstempo) file, the most recent data available at the start of this analysis. The Perstempo file contains data from the last month of every quarter from December 1987 to December 1992 and monthly data from January 1993 onward. It provides information on the MOS, unit, and grade and includes demographic characteristics, such as gender and date of birth, for all enlisted personnel and officers in the services (Army, Navy, Marine Corps, and Air Force). The source of this file is the DMDC Active Duty Master Files. The data file is structured such that each observation corresponds to an individual, who is then followed over time so that we can observe the individual throughout his or her time in the service.

MOS labels for the Army and Air Force come from the DoD Occupational Conversion Index, which is part of the Occupational Database DMDC maintains. This index includes the DoD occupational grouping, service, MOS, and service occupational title. A Marine Corps representative provided the labels for that service's occupations. A Navy representative confirmed the information in our previous report and, in some cases, provided updated information about newly opened ratings, Navy Enlisted Classifications (NECs), and designators (the Navy equivalent of enlisted and officer MOS, respectively). In some instances, open occupations are unit specific. For the present report, we restrict analyses to occupations that are not unit specific.

The Unit Identification Code (UIC) is a six-character alphanumeric code that uniquely identifies each Active, Reserve, and National Guard unit of the Armed Forces. A master file that DMDC maintains provided labels and addresses for the UICs for each service.

Navy representatives also provided us with information on the percentage of female and total slots on previously opened and newly opened ships, total slots on ships opened to women but not yet reconfigured to accommodate them, and total positions on ships still closed to women.

The services provided information on the status of individual occupations and units. When possible, service representatives confirmed that the status of individual occupations listed in the earlier RAND report (Harrell and Miller, 1997) is still current. Because the prior RAND report did not include information on the status of units at the level of detail we used in the current effort, we relied on service representatives to gather this information. In one case, the decentralized nature of the services' information system made this prohibitively burdensome and time consuming: We were not able to obtain a list of previously closed units from the Army. In such instances as these, we classified units according to the information we did receive. For the Army, we were unable to distinguish between newly open and previously open units.

Navy representatives confirmed the status of ratings, designators, NECs, and ship types presented in the previous publication. Unfortunately, the tight integration of occupations and units made it difficult for Navy representatives to provide information about the status of spaces at the UIC level (just at the level of ship types). In addition to not being able to examine the representation of women by UIC, we were also unable to distinguish open and closed occupations that depend on ship or unit type. For example, we classified all support personnel assigned to some naval special warfare units as being in open positions (unless the particular NEC or rating is always closed regardless of group or ship type) because we could not distinguish naval special warfare units from other types of units.

The service representatives confirmed the statuses of MOSs and UICs presented in previous publications and provided us with current information on the statuses of occupations and units.

Our methodological approach was as follows:

1. We calculated a subgroup mean (or percentage female) and standard error for each MOS and unit subgroup (by service and by enlisted or officer status).

2. Next, we calculated an adjusted overall mean that subtracted from the total sample the people in the particular MOS or unit being compared to the overall mean. If we allowed these people to be double counted in the subgroup and overall mean, the resulting standard errors would be too large.

3. We also corrected for the subgroup standard errors by taking the square root of the sum of the squares of the overall standard error and subgroup standard error. The uncorrected standard errors are smaller than the corrected standard errors and hence provided a more liberal test of the significance of differences between overall and subgroup means.

4. We constructed the 95-percent confidence interval for each adjusted overall mean (corresponding to a particular MOS or unit) by multiplying the corrected subgroup standard error by ±1.96.

5. We evaluated whether each subgroup mean fell within the corresponding confidence interval for the adjusted overall mean. If the subgroup was below the 95-percent confidence interval, we concluded that women are underrepresented relative to their overall representation. If the MOS or UIC percentage was above the 95-percent confidence interval, we concluded that women are overrepresented relative to their overall representation in that service.

While it is analytically useful to identify occupations that have markedly fewer (or more) women than the service overall, we are not asserting that each occupation should have the same representation as its service. Given the importance of time in the closed systems of military careers, we assert that this statistical "underrepresentation" or "overrepresentation" should be considered only as a benchmarking data point for comparison with future studies. Integration targets are discussed in more detail in the ensuing chapters.

With the exception of the Army, we classify warrant officers with all other officers. The Navy and Marines have too few warrant officers (and the Air Force has none) to merit a separate category for the purposes of examining representation of women across occupations and units.

Phase Two

The second phase of this effort focuses on selected occupations determined during the course of Phase 1. These occupations were selected to include nontraditional officer and enlisted positions, to represent all four services, to include occupations with both high and low gender representation and also to include different kinds of occupational areas.

In the course of this research, the third quarter 1999 Perstempo file was released, and we used it to update the counts for the selected occupations. When describing and summarizing issues for each of the selected occupations, we often used service-provided data, which are identified as such in this report.

Chapter Two

DATA ANALYSIS: SUMMARY OF REPRESENTATION OF WOMEN IN THE SERVICES

This chapter compares the four services in terms of representation of women overall and across specific occupations and units. The tables in this chapter summarize the larger and more comprehensive tables in the companion volume (Beckett and Chien, 2002).

GENDER REPRESENTATION ACROSS THE SERVICES

This report addresses gender representation in military occupations but does not attempt to determine the correct level of representation. Absent high-level guidance from Congress, policymakers, or the military services, it is unclear what the integration target should be. Should the occupations open to women all be integrated to the same extent? This hardly seems like a logical approach. There are occupations with assignment restrictions for women, and there are occupations, such as nursing, that have traditionally included relatively high numbers of women. Thus, absent any policy or legal guidance about integration targets, this work compares the level of representation to that of the appropriate service and notes where differences in representation are statistically significant, without necessarily meaning to imply that such differences have policy significance.

Representation levels differ among occupations for multiple reasons. A primary factor is time elapsed; it does require a full career cycle to completely integrate an occupation. Nonetheless, these data indicate a range of integration progress. Determining the specific reasons for the level of gender representation in any particular occupation requires additional qualitative analysis, such as that in Chapter

Three. Regardless, the statistical analysis suggested which occupations would be the best candidates for such further analysis and also provided a catalog of current progress to be used as a benchmark for future analysis.

Table 2.1 shows the percentage of enlisted personnel, officers, and (for the Army) warrant officers in the Army, Marine Corps, Navy, and Air Force and for all four services combined. Overall, 14 percent of enlisted personnel and officers are women. The Marines have a significantly lower representation of women, with the percentage ranging from 5 to 6 percent of all enlisted personnel and officers. The other three services have about approximately the same percentage of women, with the Air Force reporting the highest percentages (16 percent of enlisted personnel and 18 percent of officers).

OCCUPATIONS AND UNITS CLOSED TO WOMEN

Table 2.2 shows the number of positions in occupations that are closed to women. The percentage of occupations closed across services varies considerably, reflecting differences across services in the proportion of occupations that engage in direct combat or that collocate with direct combat units. The companion volume lists all occupations closed to women (Beckett and Chien, 2002, Tables D.1 through D.4), as well as the units closed to women for the Army and Marines (Beckett and Chien, 2002, Tables D.7 and D.8). The number of positions in occupations closed in the Navy underestimates the

Table 2.1

Female Personnel

Service	Officers		Enlisted		Warrant Officers	
	%	Total Number	%	Total Number	%	Total Number
Army	14.74	65,981	15.17	396,152	6.70	11,491
Navy	14.32	53,893	13.16	314,272	—[a]	
Air Force	16.8	70,320	18.83	286,170	N/A	
Marine Corps	4.90	17,894	6.00	154,830	—[a]	
Total	14.48		14.29		—	

SOURCE: Third quarter 1999 Perstempo file.
[a]Navy and Marine Corps officer numbers include warrant officers.

Table 2.2

Number of Positions in Occupations
Closed to Women

Service	Officers	Enlisted	Warrant Officers
Army	8,318	114,782	557
Air Force	61	1,623	N/A
Marine Corps	2,623	28,187	—[a]

SOURCE: Third quarter 1999 Perstempo file.

NOTE: Navy data not included here because, by nature, it requires a ship-by-ship analysis for each occupation.

[a]Marine Corps officer numbers include warrant officers.

actual number of closed positions because, in the Navy, the status of a position depends on the occupation and the ship type.[1] For instance, a particular officer occupation might be open on amphibious warfare ships but closed on submarines, because women cannot be assigned to submarines. However, since the occupation is open on some ship types but not others, the occupation is classified as "open." Thus, most officer occupations will be classified as open.

OCCUPATIONS NEWLY OPENED TO WOMEN

The central objective of this report is to evaluate the representation of women in newly opened occupations and units. Tables 2.3 through 2.6 present the newly opened occupations for each of the services, including the number of women in each newly opened occupation as of the end of 1998, the total number of personnel, and the percentage female. Each table notes whether the newly opened occupations are enlisted, officer, or warrant officer positions. Each table also characterizes the newly opened occupations by DoD occupational group (e.g., Tactical Operations Officers) and summarizes the representation in the newly opened occupations by these groupings.

---

[1]The following ship types remain closed to women in the Navy: submarines, mine-countermeasure ships, mine-hunter craft, and patrol craft. Some other ships remain functionally closed because of the costs associated with reconfiguring ships.

Table 2.3

Newly Opened Occupations, Army

	Code	Description	Women %[a]	Women Number	Total Personnel
Enlisted					
Infantry, Gun Crews, and Seamanship Specialists	12C	Bridge Crewmember	5.3*[b]	40	756
	12Z	Combat Engineer	0.0*[b]	0	352
		Subtotal	3.8*[b]	42	1,108
Other Technical and Allied Specialists	82C	Field Artillery Surveyor	7.2*[b]	64	888
		Total enlisted	5.3*[b]	106	1,996
Warrant Officers					
Tactical Operations Officers	152B	OH-58 A/C Scout Pilot	2.3*[b]	4	173
	152D	OH-58D Scout Pilot	2.5*[b]	15	570
	152F	AH-64 Pilot	1.1*[b]	9	826
	152G	AH-1 Pilot	1.2*[b]	1	83
		Total warrant officers	1.8*[b]	29	1,652

SOURCE: First quarter 1998 Perstempo file; 12C data from U.S. Army.
[a]Asterisk indicates significant at $p < 0.05$ level.
[b]Representation is lower than the group mean.

Table 2.4

Newly Opened Occupations, Navy

	Code	Description	Women %[a]	Women Number	Total Personnel
Enlisted					
Infantry, Gun Crews, and Seamanship Specialists	GM	Gunner's Mate	1.6*[b]	70	4,402
	GMG	Gunner's Mate—Guns	0.0*[b]	0	6
	GMM	Gunner's Mate—Missiles	0.0	0	1
		Subtotal	1.6*[b]	70	4,409
Electronic Equipment Repairers	FC	Fire Controlman	3.0*[b]	182	6,129
	STG	Sonar Technician—Surface	8.9*[b]	354	3,995
		Subtotal	5.3*[b]	536	10,124
Communications and Intelligence Specialists	AW	Aviation Warfare System Operator	2.2*[b]	54	2,445
	EW	Electronic Warfare Technician	4.9*[b]	93	1,889
		Subtotal	3.4*[b]	147	4,334
Electrical/Mechanical Equipment Repairers	ABE	Recovery	2.8*[b]	53	1,824
	GS	Gas Turbine System Technician	0.4*[b]	1	255
	GSE	Gas Turbine System Technician—Electrical	2.5*[b]	44	1,677

Table 2.4—Continued

| Code | Description | Women | | Total |
		%[a]	Number	Personnel
GSM	Gas Turbine System Technician—Mechanical	2.5*[b]	87	3,231
	Subtotal	2.4*[b]	132	6,987
	Total, enlisted	4.0	938	25,944

SOURCE: First quarter 1998 Perstempo file.
[a]Asterisk indicates significant at $p < 0.05$ level.
[b]Representation is lower than the group mean.

Table 2.5

Newly Opened Occupations, Air Force

	Code	Description	Women %[a]	Women Number	Total Personnel
Officers					
Tactical Operations Officers	11BXA	Bomber Pilot, B-1	2.3*[b]	5	222
	11BXC	Bomber Pilot, B-52	0.0*[b]	0	221
	11FXB	Fighter Pilot, A-10	1.1*[b]	4	377
	11FXF	Fighter Pilot, F-15	0.8*[b]	6	717
	11FXG	Fighter Pilot, F-15E	0.9*[b]	3	347
	11FXH	Fighter Pilot, F-16	0.5*[b]	7	1,350
	11SXC	Special Operations Pilot, AC-130H	3.0*[b]	1	33
	11SXF	Special Operations Pilot, MC-130E	4.2*[b]	1	24
	11SXG	Special Operations Pilot, MC-130H	0.0*[b]	0	70
	12BXA	Bomber Navigator, B-1 Defensive Systems Officer EWO	2.7*[b]	1	36
	12BXB	Bomber Navigator, Offensive Systems Officer	0.0*[b]	0	39
	12BXC	Bomber Navigator, B-1 WSO	2.6*[b]	4	148
	12FXF	Fighter Navigator, F-15E WSO	1.8*[b]	5	285
	12FXG	Fighter Navigator, F-15E EWO	0.0*[b]	0	5
	12SXH	Special Operations Navigator, MC-130E EWO	0.0*[b]	0	15

Table 2.5—Continued

Code	Description	Women		Total Personnel
		%[a]	Number	
12SXJ	Special Operations Navigator, MC-130E EWO	0.0*[b]	0	25
12SXK	Special Operations Navigator, MC-130H EWO	0.0*[b]	0	42
12SXL	Special Operations Navigator, MC-130H	0.0*[b]	0	39
Total officers		0.9*[b]	37	3,995

SOURCE: First quarter 1998 Perstempo file.
[a]Asterisk indicates significant at $p < 0.05$ level.
[b]Representation is lower than the group mean.

Table 2.6

Newly Opened Occupations, Marine Corps

	Code	Description	Women		Total
			%[a]	Number	Personnel
Enlisted					
Infantry, Gun Crews, and Seamanship Specialists	0481	Landing Support Specialist	2.8*[b]	19	658
	1371	Combat Engineer	1.5*[b]	32	2,136
	7372	First Navigator	2.6	2	75
		Subtotal	1.8*[b]	53	2,869
Electronic Equipment Repairers	5937	Aviation Radio Repairer	2.6	3	101
	5939	Aviation Radio Technician	6.1	3	49
	5942	Aviation Radar Repairer (AN/TPS-59)	3.0	6	110
	5948	Aviation Radar Technician	6.1	2	56
	6315	A/C Comm./ Navigation/Electrical Systems Technician, AV-8	4.1	8	195
	6322	Aircraft Comm./ Navigation/Electrical Systems Technician, CH-46	2.5*[b]	8	313

Table 2.6—Continued

Code	Description	Women %[a]	Women Number	Total Personnel
6323	Aircraft Comm./ Navigation/Electrical Systems Technician, CH-53	4.8	19	395
6324	Aircraft Comm./ Navigation/Electrical Systems Technician, U/AH-1	5.4	21	388
	Subtotal	4.4	70	1,607
Communications and Intelligence Specialists				
2671	Arabic Cryptologic Linguist	7.8	6	77
7242	Air Support Operations Operator	17.1*[c]	28	164
	Subtotal	14.1*[c]	34	241
Other Technical and Allied Specialists				
2336	Explosive Ordnance Disposal Technician	0.4*[b]	1	243
Electrical Mechanical Equipment Repairers				
6015	Aircraft Mechanic, AV-8/TAV-8	1.3*[b]	6	454
6055	Aircraft Airframe Mechanic, AV-8/ TAV-8	0.9*[b]	2	227

Table 2.6—Continued

	Code	Description	Women %[a]	Women Number	Total Personnel
	6112	Helicopter Mechanic, CH-46	2.1*[b]	11	520
	6113	Helicopter Mechanic, CH-53	1.8*[b]	8	446
	6114	Helicopter Mechanic, U/AH-1	2.3*[b]	10	441
	6119	Helicopter/Tiltrotor Maintenance Chief	0.0*[b]	0	86
	6135	Aircraft Power Plants Test Cell Operator, Rotary Wing/Tiltrotor	0.0*[b]	0	23
	6154	Helicopter Airframe Mechanic, A/UH-1	1.4*[b]	6	425
		Subtotal	1.6*[b]	43	2,622
		Total Enlisted	2.6*[b]	201	7,582
Officers					
Tactical Operations Officer	1302	Engineer Officer	4.7	14	300
	5702	Nuclear, Biological & Chemical Defense Officer	1.1*[b]	1	87
	7210	Air Defense Control Officer	9.4	10	106

Table 2.6—Continued

Code	Description	Women %[a]	Women Number	Total Personnel
7380	Mission Specialist/Navigation Officer	0.0*[b]	0	14
7507	FRS Basic AV-8B Pilot	0.0*[b]	0	30
7509	Pilot VMA-AV-8B	0.0*[b]	0	269
7511	Pilot VMA (AW) A-6	0.0	0	1
7521	FRS Basic F/A-18 Pilot	0.0*[b]	0	50
7523	Pilot VMFA F/A-18	0.0*[b]	0	402
7524	FRS Basic F/A-18D Weapons Sensors Officer	0.0*[b]	0	13
7525	F/A-18D WSO	0.0*[b]	0	148
7527	Pilot VMFA F/A-18D Qualified	0.0	0	1
7541	FRS Basic EA-6B Pilot	0.0	0	1
7543	Pilot VMAQ/EA-6B	0.0*[b]	0	58
7551	Pilot C-9	0.0*[b]	0	3
7555	Pilot, UC-12B	0.0*[b]	0	11
7556	KC-130 Co-Pilot (T2P/T3P)	1.0*[b]	1	100
7557	KC-130 Aircraft Commander	0.0*[b]	0	118

Table 2.6—Continued

Code	Description	Women		Total Personnel
		%[a]	Number	
7558	FRS Basic CH-53D Pilot	33.3	1	3
7559	Pilot CT-39	0.0*b	0	5
7560	FRS Basic CH-53E Pilot	0.0*b	0	28
7561	FRS Basic CH-46 Pilot	0.0*b	0	16
7562	Pilot HMH/M/L/ A CH-46	0.5*b	3	590
7563	Pilot HMH/M/L/ A UH-1	0.5*b	1	203
7564	CH-53 A/D Qualified	0.8*b	1	129
7565	Pilot HMH/M/L/A AH-1	0.0*b	0	318
7566	Pilot HMH CH-53E	1.0*b	3	301
7567	FRS UH-1N Pilot	0.0*b	0	12
7568	FRS Basic AH-1 Pilot	0.0*b	0	26
7577	Weapons & Tactics Instructor	0.0*b	0	4
7591	Naval Flight Officer (VMAW)	0.0	0	2
7595	Test Pilot/Flight Test Project Officer	0.0*b	0	8
7598	Basic Fixed Wing Pilot	0.0*b	0	63
	Subtotal	1.0*b	35	3,420

Table 2.6—Continued

	Code	Description	Women		Total Personnel
			%[a]	Number	
Engineering and Maintenance Officers		Explosive Ordnance			
	2305	Disposal Officer	0.0*[b]	0	35
	7596	Aviation Safety Officer	0.0*[b]	0	25
		Subtotal	0.0*[b]	0	60
Supply, Procurement and Allied Officers	1390	Bulk Fuel Officer	0.0*[b]	0	29
Nonoccupational	7599	Flight Student	3.9	31	799
		Total officers	1.5	66	4,308

SOURCE: First quarter 1998 Perstempo file.
[a]Asterisk indicates significant at $p < 0.05$ level.
[b]Representation is lower than the group mean.
[c]Representation is higher than the group mean.

Table 2.7 provides the percentages of these newly opened occupations that underrepresent women relative to their level of representation among the service's officers and enlisted personnel. Most newly opened occupations have lower levels of gender representation than the service overall. In the Army, women are statistically underrepresented in each of the three newly opened enlisted MOSs and in each of the four newly opened MOSs for warrant officers. Likewise, in the Navy, women are underrepresented in ten of the eleven newly opened enlisted ratings; in the Air Force, women are underrepresented in each of the 18 newly opened occupations.

However, there are two important issues to remember when observing this phenomenon. First, even if women entered all occupations at representative levels, it would take a full career cycle—as long as 15 to 20 years in some instances—for representation in these careers to resemble that of the service overall. Indeed, some evidence indicates that women may still be in the training pipeline leading to some of these newly opened officer positions, at least in the Marine Corps. Most of the newly opened Marine officer positions are pilots. As of 1998, about 4 percent of flight students (MOS 7599) were women, which is not statistically different from the overall percentage of Marine officers who are female (5.6 percent). The absolute number of women in the newly opened MOSs among Marine pilot and naval flight officers has increased since 1996. In 1996, 29 women were in newly opened MOSs in the 7500 series (Table B.17 in Harrell and Miller, 1997), compared with 41 women as of first quarter 1998 (Table 2.6). The number of women in these positions is increasing

Table 2.7

**Newly Opened Occupations With Gender Representation
Lower Than Service Overall**

Service	Officers		Enlisted		Warrant Officers[a]	
	%	Number	%	Number	%	Number
Army	—	0	100.0	3	100.0	4
Navy	—	0	90.9	11		
Air Force	100.0	18	—	0		
Marine Corps	78.4	37	54.5	22		

SOURCE: First quarter 1998 Perstempo file.

[a]Because the Navy, Air Force, and Marine Corps have only small numbers of warrant officers, they are classified with all officers.

each year and, if the representation of women in flight school reflects the future, may achieve parity across most of these positions as women progress through the Marine pilot pipeline. Unfortunately, the limited scope of this project restricts our ability to identify comparable data trends in the other services for the newly opened positions. However, Chapter Three explores such issues for selected occupational areas.

It is not reasonable to expect the newly opened occupations to have reached representative levels already. The rate at which they might do so depends on the retention of the people already in the occupation, the rate at which women and men are entering the occupation, and the length of time the occupation has been open to women. For example, if there are 1,000 people in a career field and if people stay for an average of 15 years, the turnover is only 6.6 percent each year, and only approximately 67 people enter that career field annually. If Army enlisted women are entering this field at a representative rate (15.3 percent), approximately 11 women enter it each year. If the occupation had opened to women in 1994, not more than 77, or 7.7 percent of the total personnel in this occupation, would be female. For occupations with shorter average retention, the expected representation would be higher. Without knowing the average retention of individuals in each career and exactly when each career field opened to women, it is not possible to ascertain an expected representation level. However, many of the representation rates of the newly opened occupations, as indicated in Tables 2.3 through 2.7, appear low even given conservative assumptions.

Many of these careers are among classes of occupations that currently underrepresent women, even in occupations that were previously open to women. This suggests that women may not be entering the occupation at representative rates. The difference in levels of representation among previously open careers is apparent in Tables 2.8 through 2.11, which summarize the representation of all previously open occupations by major category (the tables are restricted to occupations with at least 10 personnel). These tables indicate that women have tended toward careers in health care, administration, and intelligence, even when careers in other areas were available.[2]

---

[2]The full (open) occupational list is shown in Tables D.9 through D.17 of Beckett and Chien (2002).

Table 2.8

Summary of Gender Representation in Previously Open Army Occupations

Description	Women %[a]	Women Number	Total Pers.
Enlisted			
Infantry, Gun Crews, and Seamanship Specialists	12.1*[b]	472	3,916
Electronic Equipment Repairers	11.1*[b]	2,887	26,058
Communications and Intelligence Specialists	20.4*[c]	5,061	24,765
Health Care Specialists	31.6*[c]	10,446	33,082
Other Technical and Allied Specialists	16.5	1,992	12,097
Functional Support and Administration	35.7*[c]	21,605	60,434
Electrical/Mechanical Equipment Repairers	9.9*[b]	4,752	48,007
Craftsworkers	11.7*[b]	908	7,743
Service and Supply Handlers	20.4*[c]	9,727	47,686
Total enlisted	21.9	57,850	263,788
Officers			
General Officers and Executives, NEC	3.5*[b]	12	346
Tactical Operations Officers	5.3*[b]	605	11,330
Intelligence Officers	16.3*[c]	540	3,307
Engineering and Maintenance Officers	15.5*[c]	782	5,044
Scientists and Professionals	9.8*[b]	447	4,550
Health Care Officers	30.7*[c]	3,752	12,223
Administrators	19.9*[c]	819	4,110
Supply, Procurement and Allied Officers	16.0*[c]	936	5,840
Nonoccupational	12.5*[b]	227	1,813
Total officers	16.7	8,120	48,563
Warrant officers			
Tactical Operations Officers	2.2*[b]	59	2,264
Intelligence Officers	13.2*[c]	116	880
Engineering and Maintenance Officers	3.3*[b]	78	2,334
Scientists and Professionals	21.3*[c]	13	61
Health Care Officers	17.8*[c]	24	135
Administrators	16.7*[c]	112	669
Supply, Procurement and Allied Officers	19.2*[c]	190	990
Total warrant officers	7.7	592	7,693

SOURCE: First quarter 1998 Perstempo file.
[a]Asterisk indicates significant at $p < 0.05$ level.
[b]Representation is lower than the group mean.
[c]Representation is higher than the group mean.

Table 2.9

Summary of Gender Representation in Previously Open Navy Occupations

Description	Women %[a]	Number	Total Pers.
Enlisted			
Infantry, Gun Crews, and Seamanship Specialists	16.5*[c]	3,470	21,053
Electronic Equipment Repairers	7.1*[b]	1,054	14,743
Communications and Intelligence Specialists	15.6*[c]	1,637	10,516
Health Care Specialists	15.9*[c]	2,514	15,766
Other Technical and Allied Specialists	14.8*[c]	209	1,415
Functional Support and Administration	18.4*[c]	1,029	5,593
Electrical/Mechanical Equipment Repairers	6.9*[b]	1,484	21,613
Craftsworkers	5.9*[b]	347	5,920
Service and Supply Handlers	11.2*[b]	492	4,382
Nonoccupational	0.0*[b]	—	15
Total enlisted	12.1	12,236	101,009
Officers			
General Officers and Executives, NEC	16.9*[c]	405	2,391
Tactical Operations Officers	4.0*[b]	520	12,911
Intelligence Officers	25.2*[c]	576	2,289
Engineering and Maintenance Officers	6.6*[b]	513	7,769
Scientists and Professionals	15.7*[c]	618	3,927
Health Care Officers	33.2*[c]	2,682	8,076
Administrators	20.0*[c]	966	4,821
Supply, Procurement and Allied Officers	10.5*[b]	244	2,882
Nonoccupational	24.0*[c]	125	520
Total officers	14.8	6,649	45,036

SOURCE: First quarter 1998 Perstempo file.
[a]Asterisk indicates significant at $p < 0.05$ level.
[b]Representation is lower than the group mean.
[c]Representation is higher than the group mean.

It is important to note that it was not possible to determine from the data the extent to which these career choices are a result of self-selection or systemic limitations. For example, recruiter and career counselor attitudes, not just technical manpower models, may influence career assignment. That is, if the models that determine which occupations are available to new recruits do not offer new female recruits the same choices they offer to males or if recruiters or guidance counselors do not encourage female recruits to accept nontraditional career areas, the expected gender representation among nontraditional career areas would be low. This project cannot fully examine the career assignment processes and models for all four services, although there is separate ongoing RAND research of the Army system.

Table 2.10

**Summary of Gender Representation in Previously
Open Air Force Occupations**

Description	Women %[a]	Number	Total Pers.
Enlisted			
Infantry, Gun Crews, and Seamanship Specialists	10.0*[b]	2,487	24,876
Electronic Equipment Repairers	7.1*[b]	1,924	27,220
Communications and Intelligence Specialists	22.6*[c]	4,824	21,346
Health Care Specialists	42.6*[c]	10,708	25,145
Other Technical and Allied Specialists	11.7*[b]	1,323	11,328
Functional Support and Administration	31.7*[c]	22,493	70,936
Electrical/Mechanical Equipment Repairers	4.0*[b]	2,705	67,417
Craftsworkers	5.4*[b]	669	12,408
Service and Supply Handlers	17.7	2,497	14,074
Nonoccupational	24.5*[c]	1,315	5,358
Total enlisted	18.2	50,945	280,108
Officers			
General Officers and Executives, NEC	3.6*[b]	32	882
Tactical Operations Officers	5.2*[b]	969	18,814
Intelligence Officers	17.7	294	1,665
Engineering and Maintenance Officers	13.7*[b]	1,178	8,573
Scientists and Professionals	15.5	787	5,089
Health Care Officers	40.9*[c]	5,222	12,779
Administrators	24.3*[c]	1,155	4,750
Supply, Procurement and Allied Officers	14.3*[b]	904	6,343
Nonoccupational	9.6*[b]	326	3,380
Total officers	17.5	10,867	62,275

SOURCE: First quarter 1998 Perstempo file.
[a]Asterisk indicates significant at $p < 0.05$ level.
[b]Representation is lower than the group mean.
[c]Representation is higher than the group mean.

Table 2.11

Summary of Gender Representation in Previously
Open Marine Corps Occupations

Description	Women %[a]	Women Number	Total Pers.
Enlisted			
Infantry, Gun Crews, and Seamanship Specialists	2.7*[b]	115	4,218
Electronic Equipment Repairers	3.9*[b]	211	5,426
Communications and Intelligence Specialists	7.1*[c]	643	9,072
Other Technical and Allied Specialists	10.3*[c]	326	3,180
Functional Support and Administration	11.0*[c]	2,827	25,781
Electrical/Mechanical Equipment Repairers	4.2*[b]	705	16,673
Craftsworkers	4.7*[b]	159	3,366
Service and Supply Handlers	6.5*[c]	1,207	18,460
Nonoccupational	8.7*[c]	823	9,450
Total enlisted	7.3	7,016	95,626
Officer			
General Officers and Executives, NEC	1.8*[b]	9	507
Tactical Operations Officers	4.1	16	394
Intelligence Officers	6.2	31	502
Engineering and Maintenance Officers	3.8	55	1,454
Scientists and Professionals	7.0*[c]	31	444
Administrators	14.2*[c]	205	1,445
Supply, Procurement and Allied Officers	7.5*[c]	149	1,992
Nonoccupational	5.5*[c]	172	3,155
Total officers	6.8	668	9,893

SOURCE: First quarter 1998 Perstempo file.
[a]Asterisk indicates significant at $p < 0.05$ level.
[b]Representation is lower than the group mean.
[c]Representation is higher than the group mean.

Tables 2.12 and 2.13 summarize the statistics on gender representation by major occupational category. For each service, these tables indicate the percentage of newly opened occupations and the percentage of previously opened occupations in each class in which women are either over- or underrepresented. A down arrow (↓) in a cell indicates that the percentage shown reflects the percentage of MOSs within the occupational category for which there is a statistically significant underrepresentation of women relative to the overall

Table 2.12

Newly Opened and Previously Opened Enlisted Occupations That Over or Underrepresent Women, 1998

Occupation Class	Army				Navy				Air Force				Marine Corps			
	Newly Open		Previously Open		Newly Open		Previously Open		Newly Open		Previously Open		Newly Open		Previously Open	
	%	No.	%	No.	%	No.	%	No.	%	No.	%	No.	%	No.	%	No.
Infantry, Gun Crews, and Seamanship Specialists	100↓	2	60↑	5	66↓	3	59↓	17	—		79↓	14	100↓	2	89↓	18
Electronic Equipment Repairers	—		50↓	28	100↓	2	54↓	157	—		98↓	46	13↓	8	35↓	54
Communications and Intelligence Specialists	—		55↑	20	100↓	2	35↑	62	—		45↑	42	50↓	2	25↑	28
Health Care Specialists	—		88↑	17	—		47↑	47	—		74↑	39	—		—	
Other Technical and Allied Specialists	100↓	1	39↑	31	—		30↓	27	—		53↓	34	100↓	1	28↑	29
Functional Support and Administration	—		86↑	21	—		55↑	42	—		49↑	51	—		64↑	33

Table 2.12—Continued

Occupation Class	Army Newly Open %	No.	Army Previously Open %	No.	Navy Newly Open %	No.	Navy Previously Open %	No.	Air Force Newly Open %	No.	Air Force Previously Open %	No.	Marine Corps Newly Open %	No.	Marine Corps Previously Open %	No.
Electrical/Mech-anical Equipment Repairers	—	—	88↓	34	100↓	4	54↓	125			100↓	61	100↓	8	63↓	60
Craftsworkers	—	—	80↓	15	—		59↓	44			80↓	15	—		36↓	11
Service and Supply Handlers	—		60↑	10	—		31↕	13		·	71↓	14	—		29↓	21
Nonoccupational	—		—		—		100↓	1			13↕	8	—		50↑	8

NOTES: Previously opened occupations restricted to those with at least 10 personnel. A down arrow (↓) indicates that the percentage shown reflects the percentage of MOSs within the occupational category for which there is a statistically significant underrepresentation of women relative to the service-specific overall percentage female. An up arrow (↑) indicates that the percentage refers to the percentage of MOSs that overrepresent women. If both arrows appear, the same percentage of occupations within the class overrepresent women as underrepresent them.

Table 2.13

Newly Opened and Previously Opened Officer Occupations That Over or Underrepresent Women, 1998

Occupation Class	Army				Navy				Air Force				Marine Corps			
	Newly Open		Previously Open		Newly Open		Previously Open		Newly Open		Previously Open		Newly Open		Previously Open	
	%	No.	%	No.	%	No.	%	No.	%	No.	%	No.	%	No.	%	No.
General Officers and Executives, NEC	—		100↓	1	—		39↓	23	—		100↓	5	—		60↓	5
Tactical Operations Officers	100↓	4	80↓	10	—		79↓	97	100↓	18	87↓	135	81↓	33	29↓	7
Intelligence Officers	—		33↕	6	—		10↕	30	—		33↕	3	—		20↓	5
Engineering and Maintenance Officers	—		23↕	13	—		56↓	113	—		55↓	22	100↓	2	32↓	22
Scientists and Professionals	—		86↓	14	—		20↓	45	—		53↓	17	—		50↓	6
Health Care Officers	—		39↑	71	—		32↑	78	—		33↕	93	—		—	
Administrators	—		38↑	13	—		35↑	57	—		35↑	17	—		32↑	19
Supply, Procurement and Allied Officers	—		36↑	11	—		29↓	31	—		50↓	10	100↓	1	29↓	14
Nonoccupational	—		100↓	1	—		100↑	2	—		60↓	5	100↓	1	50↓	6

NOTES: Previously opened occupations restricted to those with at least 10 personnel. Army "Newly Open" column shows warrant officers. A down arrow (↓) indicates that the percentage shown reflects the percentage of MOSs within the occupational category for which there is a statistically significant underrepresentation of women relative to the service-specific overall percentage female. An up arrow (↑) indicates that the percentage refers to the percentage of MOSs that overrepresent women. If both arrows appear, the same percentage of occupations within the class overrepresent women as underrepresent them.

percentage of women within the specific service. Conversely, an up arrow (↑) denotes that the percentage shown refers to the percentage of MOSs that overrepresent women. For example, the first occupational class in Table 2.12 is Infantry, Gun Crews, and Seamanship Specialists; the arrows in the Army columns indicate that 100 percent of the two newly open occupations in this class and 60 percent of the five previously open occupations underrepresent women. The important point to note from these tables is that, in the majority of cases, the same occupational classes tend to have relatively high or low levels of gender representation, regardless of whether they are newly opened or had been previously opened.

DIFFERENCES IN REPRESENTATION ACROSS GRADES

Because the data analyzed in this chapter are cross-sectional, rather than longitudinal, it was difficult to capture trends in occupational assignment. Nonetheless, it is still useful to capture the level of gender representation in the different career areas by grade. Given correct assumptions, looking at representation by junior and senior ranks will identify some basic trends worthy of further examination. Table 2.14 compares the occupational breakdown for female junior officers to that for female senior officers. These data address the issue of whether female accessions are entering the same career areas today that they have in the past. In general, a higher percentage of female junior officers are tactical operations officers and engineering and maintenance officers, and slightly fewer are in administrative jobs. The largest portion of female officers remains in the health care professions.

Table 2.15 presents comparable data for enlisted women. Although junior enlisted women in all the services are much less represented in the administrative careers than are more-senior enlisted women, the details are otherwise different for the different services. In the Army, there have been increases in Service and Supply Handlers, Electrical/Mechanical Equipment Repairers, and Electronic Equipment Repairers. Navy enlisted women are now overrepresented in combat-oriented careers and have also moved into electrical and mechanical equipment repair occupations. Those data suggest that they have moved away from electronic equipment repair, communications and intelligence, and health care careers. Air Force enlisted

Table 2.14

Total Percentages of Female Junior and Senior Officer Personnel in Occupational Classes (1998)

Occupational Class	Army		Navy		Air Force		Marine Corps	
	O1–O3	O4–O6	O1–O3	O4–O6	O1–O3	O4–O6	O1–O3	O4–O6
General Officers and Executives	0	0	2	13	0	1	0	5
Tactical Operations Officers	9	4	10	5	10	8	5	3
Intelligence Officers	7	5	7	11	2	4	5	5
Engineering and Maintenance Officers	12	6	10	5	11	10	8	8
Scientists and Professionals	5	7	10	8	7	7	4	5
Health Care Officers	43	53	43	36	50	44	—	—
Administrators	9	12	12	18	10	12	29	33
Supply, Procurement and Allied Officers	12	10	4	3	7	11	23	19
Nonoccupational	3	3	2	1	3	3	26	22
Total	100	100	100	100	100	100	100	100

Table 2.15

Total Percentages of Female Junior and Senior Enlisted Personnel in Occupational Classes (1998)

Occupational Class	Army		Navy		Air Force		Marine Corps	
	E1–E4	E5–E9	E1–E4	E5–E9	E1–E4	E5–E9	E1–E4	E5–E9
Infantry, Gun Crews, and Seamanship Specialists	1	0	45	2	6	3	2	4
Electronic Equipment Repairers	6	4	7	12	4	3	4	4
Communications and Intelligence Specialists	8	10	10	20	10	8	11	7
Health Care Specialists	18	18	16	25	23	17	—	—
Other Technical and Allied Specialists	3	4	1	3	3	3	4	5
Functional Support and Administration	33	44	3	17	38	55	30	57
Electrical/Mechanical Equipment Repairers	10	6	15	9	5	6	12	6
Craftsworkers	2	1	1	5	1	1	2	2
Service and Supply Handlers	19	13	2	7	6	4	20	11
Nonoccupational	—	—	0	0	4	0	15	4
Total	100	100	100	100	100	100	100	100

women are even more highly represented in health care careers. Most of the increases among enlisted female Marines have been in Service and Supply Handlers, Electrical/Mechanical Equipment Repair, and Communications and Intelligence career classes.

It is important to note some shortcomings of this static snapshot of representation in occupations by grade. We have used these data as a proxy for a longitudinal assessment to compare the different career areas of women who entered the service more recently with those having longer tenure. However, we are unable to discern from this data whether female personnel in different occupations have different retention patterns and thus cannot determine whether it is problematic to make this kind of comparison. Also, some career areas may have disproportionate numbers of positions at junior grades or at senior grades. Given these concerns, Chapter Three further addresses the grade distributions and the trends in accessions for selected occupations.

UNITS NEWLY OPENED TO WOMEN

So far, the discussion has focused on gender representation by occupation. Information on the representation of women in newly opened units is spottier than occupation-specific data. All Air Force units were opened to women before the 1992–1994 legislative and policy changes. The Marine Corps is currently reassessing the units that are open to women, with the likelihood of changes. Some of the Army units newly opened to women are as small as platoons, and data are not readily available to assess the assignment of women to such units. We attempted to analyze gender assignment to Army and Marine Corps units by six-digit UIC but were stymied by data complications that suggested that UIC coding is not reliable. Thus, Chapter Three will address issues regarding unit assignment by gender for the selected occupations.

REPRESENTATION OF WOMEN ON NAVY SHIPS

The Secretary of the Defense's guidance of April 28, 1993 (Aspin, 1993) and the repeal of the combat exclusion resulted in the opening up of ship assignments to women for most types of ships (Harrell and Miller, 1997).[3] In 1997, women held 6 percent of enlisted slots and 12 percent of officer slots on newly opened ships. Representation of women among officers is higher than among enlisted because of the berthing requirements. Officer assignments are flexible (and gender-neutral, except for the ship types that are closed to women) because the officer accommodations could in many cases be easily modified. Modifications require both berthing and head facilities. For officers, berthing requirements in many cases were very minor, as officers are berthed mostly in double rooms. Where multiple officer heads were available, one was designated as the female head. In other situations, officers shared the single head and used a "flip sign" that designated current use. In contrast, berthing requirements for enlisted personnel required significant modification to accommodate women. Because of these structural difficulties, some ships have not been modified before their decommissioning.

As a result of the 1993 changes, the Navy developed an embarkation plan that specified the timeline by which specific ships were to be modified to accommodate female crew members. The embarkation plan was designed to coincide with the existing overhaul schedule, and thus the modifications were planned to occur when ships were normally scheduled for overhaul. This approach prevented disruption of ships' operational schedules and was less expensive than a separate modification schedule would have been. While the embarkation plan slowed the integration of women onto ships, it meant that the Navy could assign women to ships *en masse* and could assign female officers and female chief petty officers before assigning female junior enlisted personnel. While this plan limited the number of women being recruited in the Navy in the early years of the embarkation plan, the expectation was that this limitation would be short-lived and would be resolved as the transition period ended (set for FY 2003).

---

[3]The ship types added in April 1993 were fast combat support ships, replenishment oilers (AOR), amphibious command ships (LCC), auxiliary command ships (AGF), and fleet staff (2,3,7). Ship types added when combat exclusion was repealed were cruisers (CG), destroyers (DD/DDG), frigates (FF/FFG), amphibious warfare ships (LHA/LHD/LPD/LSD/LST), mine countermeasure command and control ships (MCS), and aircraft carriers (CV/CVN).

Table 2.16 indicates the representation, as of December 2000, onboard ships that had been open to women before 1994. Almost one-fourth of the enlisted personnel on these ships are female service members.

Table 2.17 summarizes personnel assignments to ships that had been opened to women as of 1994 and that had already been structurally modified by December 2000.[4] This table lists, by ship class, the number of ships included and the number of positions, by gender for male and female personnel. The representation of women on these ships overall is lower than on previously opened ships, but DMDC's most recent estimates indicate that the representation of women on both previously and newly opened ships is higher than in the Navy overall. As of December 2000, the DoD Active Duty Profile Report shows that, in the Navy, 13.8 percent of enlisted personnel and 14.7 percent of officers are women. Current representation onboard integrated combatant ships is also higher than that recorded as of April 1997 in the prior RAND study (Table B.12 in Harrell and Miller, 1997), when only 6 percent of enlisted personnel, 12 percent of officers, and 7 percent of total personnel on ships were women.

Almost all surface ships, with the exception of patrol craft, are technically open to women. While ship reconfiguration has generally been necessary for female enlisted personnel to serve on combatant ships, this is considerably less of an issue for female officers, because officer berthing and accommodations are generally more flexible. Table 2.18 shows the ships that are open to women but have not yet been structurally modified. The long-range embarkation plan is currently being revisited. For now, however, approximately 31,277 enlisted slots and 2,842 officer slots (with some exceptions noted in the table) are closed to women until structural modification, although female officers do serve on ships that are not available for female enlisted members.

Table 2.19 lists the number of billets that are not open to women. The majority of these assignments are on submarines. The Navy

---

[4]More detailed information, by individual ship, can be found in the companion volume (Beckett and Chien, 2002).

Table 2.16

Gender-Integrated Navy Ships Opened to Women Before 1994 (December 2000)

| Ship Identification | | | Enlisted | | | Officers | | | Crew Overall | | |
Class	ID	Name	Male	Female	% Female	Male	Female	% Female	Male	Female	% Female
AS	39	Emory S. Land	806	462	36	78	5	6	884	467	35
AS	40	Frank Cable	950	320	25	77	4	5	1,027	324	24
AOE	1	Sacramento	511	91	15	29	5	15	1,208	96	15
AOE	2	Camden	484	143	23	47	5	10	1,131	148	22
AOE	3	Seattle	628	84	12	40	3	7	668	87	12
AOE	4	Detroit	555	123	18	45	3	6	600	126	17
ARS	50	Safeguard	69	23	25	5	2	29	74	25	25
ARS	51	Grasp	47	45	49	N/A	N/A	N/A	47	45	49
ARS	52	Salvor	67	25	27	N/A	N/A	N/A	67	25	27
ARS	53	Grapple	58	34	37	6	1	14	64	35	35
		Total	4,175	1,350	24	327	28	8	5,656	1,308	22

SOURCE: U.S. Navy.

Table 2.17

Gender-Integrated Navy Ships Opened to Women 1994 or Later (December 2000)

Ship Class	No. Ships	Enlisted			Officers			Crews for Ship Class Overall		
		Male	Female	% Female	Male	Female	% Female	Male	Female	% Female
CV	1	4,753	293	5.8	568	10	1.7	5,321	303	5.4
CVN	10	50,819	5,893	10.4	3,658	147	3.9	54,477	6,040	10.0
CG	11	3,118	493	13.7	265	65	19.7	3,057	543	15.1
DD	18	4,212	1,167	21.7	426	87	17.0	4,638	1254	21.3
DDG	20	5,190	1,260	19.5	433	87	16.7	5,623	1,347	19.3
LCC	2	1,969	287	12.7	461	8	1.7	2,430	295	10.8
LHA	3	2,296	454	16.5	234	28	10.7	2,530	482	16.0
LHD	6	4,484	1570	25.9	389	49	11.2	4,873	1,619	24.9
LPD	1	386	73	16.0	N/A	N/A	N/A	386	73	16.0
LSD	12	3,541	1,175	24.9	208	56	21.2	3,749	1,231	24.7
AGF	2	1,062	131	11.0	154	18	10.5	1,216	149	10.9
AOE	2	1,091	235	17.7	85	5	5.6	1,176	240	16.9
Active Reserve Ships										
MCS	1	559	124	18.1	55	6	9.8	614	130	17.5
LST	1	175	34	16.2	9	3	25.0	184	37	16.7
MHC	2	67	25	27.1	N/A	N/A	N/A	67	25	27.1
Total	90	83,722	1,321	13.6	6,945	569	7.6	89,888	13,670	13.2

SOURCE: U.S. Navy.

Table 2.18

Nonintegrated Navy Ships Open to Women
(December 2000)

Class	Number of Ships	Male Enlisted	Male Officer	Female Officer
CV	1	5,049	578	11
CG	17	5,587	561	16
DD	4	1,163	101	6
DDG	11	3,465	286	15
FFG	28	5,552	520	2
LHA	2	1,831	184	12
LPD	10	4,142	252	12
LSD	3	1,188	78	2
MCM	9	675	54	0
MHC	2	92	10	0
Active Reserve Ships				
FFG	8	1,581	136	1
LST	1	209	12	5
MCM	5	375	30	0
MHC	8	368	40	1
Total	109	31,277	2,842	83

SOURCE: U.S. Navy.

Table 2.19

Patrol Craft and Submarine Billets Closed to Women
(December 2000)

Class	Identification	Total Ships in Class	Total Billets Enlisted[a]	Total Billets Officer[a]
PC	2-14	13	299	65
SSBN	726-743	18	5,040	540
SSN	21-23	3	363	39
SSN	640	1[b]	107	13
SSN	683 & 686	2	280	30
SSN	688-775	55	6,655	715
	Total		12,744	1,402

SOURCE: U.S. Navy.
[a]All male.
[b]Precommissioning.

kept submarines and small ships (mine countermeasures, mine-hunting craft, and patrol craft) closed because of prohibitive berthing and privacy issues.

In summary, the Navy has made marked progress in integrating women aboard previously and recently opened ships since 1997. Women's representation on previously open and newly open ships (ships that have been structurally modified) is greater than their representation in the Navy overall. However, 35 percent of enlisted slots on ships and 30 percent of officer slots on ships remain closed to women (with some exceptions among the officer slots) because some ships have not yet been structurally modified or because there are no plans to do so (in the case of submarines and other small vessels). Far more slots are unavailable for the former reason.

SUMMARY

These data indicate that women are not represented in newly opened occupations at levels comparable to their overall representation in their respective services. This may be reasonable, given the limited time that has elapsed. However, the various occupations indicate different levels of integration. Career-length patterns and other occupation-specific information are necessary to calculate expected levels of representation more precisely, and we will address this further in the next chapter for selected occupations. Absent more detailed information for each of the occupations addressed quantitatively in this chapter, this information is best used as a benchmark for further analysis.

It is also worthy of note that some newly opened occupations are similar to (i.e., included in the same occupational class as) occupations previously open to women, and some of the previously opened occupations also have low levels of representation. Thus, it is not clear to what extent gender representation reflects personal choice or systemic hindrances to women interested in less-traditional career areas. On the other hand, our snapshot of the representation of junior and senior women in the services suggests that junior women may be entering previously opened occupations that have traditionally underrepresented women. We cannot say whether this means that more younger women are entering these occupations, indicates differential attrition rates by sex, or simply reflects the greater representation of women in the services in general over time, but we will attempt to address some of these possible explanations in the next chapter.

Chapter Three

EXAMINATION OF SELECTED OCCUPATIONS

This chapter summarizes the results of the second task of this study by addressing the gender representation of selected newly opened occupations to improve understanding of accession, training, and retention because these processes all contribute to gender representation and to assess whether there are systemic hindrances to career development. The occupations were selected to include nontraditional officer and enlisted occupations, to represent all four services, to include occupations with both high and low gender representation, and to include different kinds of occupational areas. The next section provides the occupations included in this chapter and describes the issues discussed for each selected occupation. The chapter then addresses each of the selected occupations.

SELECTED OCCUPATIONS

The intent of this research is to examine approximately two occupations for each of the four services to sample the policies and practices regarding gender integration in newly opened occupations. Table 3.1 lists the occupations selected for examination. All but one are newly opened occupations, and thus officers and enlisted personnel are not both included for each of the services.

Table 3.1 indicates two Army enlisted and one Army warrant officer occupation. One of the enlisted careers, Bridge Crewmember, is appealing because it represents an occupational class that, as was shown in Table 2.12, traditionally underrepresents women. Additionally, because Bridge Crewmember is part of the Combat Engi-

Table 3.1

Occupations Selected for Further Analysis

Service	Enlisted or Officer	Occupation Code	Occupation Description	Occupational Class	% Female	Total Personnel
Army	Enlisted	12C	Bridge Crewmember	Infantry, Gun Crews, and Seamanship Specialists	5.3	756
Army	Enlisted	82C	Field Artillery Surveyor	Other Technical and Allied Specialists	7.2	888
Army	Warrant officer	152F	AH-64 Pilot	Tactical Operations Officers	1.1	826
Navy	Enlisted	GM	Gunner's Mate	Infantry, Gun Crews, and Seamanship Specialists	1.6	4,402
Navy	Enlisted	STG	Sonar Technician—Surface	Electronic Equipment Repairers	8.9	3,995
Navy	Officer	SWO	Surface Warfare Officer	Tactical Operations	5.0	6,361
Air Force	Officer		Fighter Pilot, F-16	Tactical Operations	0.5	1,350
Marine Corps	Enlisted	1371	Combat Engineer	Infantry, Gun Crews, and Seamanship Specialists	1.5	2,136
Marine Corps	Enlisted	7242	Air Support Operations Operator	Communications and Intelligence Specialists	17.7	164
Marine Corps	Officer	7523	Pilot F/A-18	Tactical Operations Officers	0.0	402

SOURCES: First quarter 1998 Perstempo file. FY 1998 surface warfare data provided by the surface warfare community.

neering career management field, there may be interesting parallels with the Marine Corps Combat Engineer occupation. The second Army occupation, Field Artillery Surveyor, has lower levels of gender representation than the overall Army but does have a higher representation than any of the other newly opened occupations. It represents an occupational class that traditionally overrepresents Army women. The Army warrant officer occupation suggested is the largest of the newly opened warrant officer pilot occupations.

Two of the Navy occupations selected are relatively large enlisted occupations in career areas that are not traditional choices for women. Although the two selected occupations are similar in size, they exhibited very different levels of representation as of 1998: 1.6 percent for Gunner's Mate and 8.9 percent for Sonar Technician-Surface (STG). Understanding the differences between these two newly opened occupations is very compelling. There were no newly opened Navy occupations for naval officers, but we included Surface Warfare Officer (SWO) in this analysis to address naval officer opportunities. Although this career area had previously been open to women, the opportunities for women changed dramatically when combatant ships were opened to women.

The Air Force occupation—F-16 Fighter Pilot—is one of the most visible occupations in the Air Force and the largest career field among the newly opened Air Force occupations.

The Marine Corps officer occupation is associated with another well-known aircraft, and only one woman is currently assigned to it. The selection of the Combat Engineering occupation was discussed above. The remaining Marine Corps enlisted occupation is Air Support Operations, which, as of 1998, had the highest level of female representation among all the newly opened occupations in all the services.

VALUE AND LIMITATIONS OF A CASE STUDY APPROACH

This analysis looks only at a small number of occupations. We cannot, therefore, use it to form judgments about the progress of integration throughout all occupations or to predict accurately the eventual outcome of integration even in the occupations selected. Instead, analyzing such a small subset in detail provides insights through the similarities and differences that emerge. For example, the extent to which the services constrain the number of female accessions appears to play a larger role in the integration of the selected occupations than does the nature of the work itself. Thus, one Marine Corps officer's comment that "after all the research is done and the experts have weighed in, women still do not like to turn wrenches, sleep in the mud, or kick boxes" is not reflected in the data for these occupations.

ISSUES ADDRESSED FOR SELECTED OCCUPATIONS

This research attempted to provide or address the following for each of the selected occupations:

- a description of the occupation, including the main tasks performed, the level of technical or other expertise required, and the perceived status of this career field
- the circumstances surrounding the opening of that career area (by law or by policy)
- whether there are similar occupations (in any service)
- how individuals are accessed, including prerequisites or other selection restrictions
- whether there is evidence that recruiters and the models they use encourage or discourage female assignment to these occupations (to be determined through recruiting and manpower policy professionals)
- retention rates, by gender
- training requirements and attrition information, by gender, for the training period
- typical assignment patterns throughout the career and the degree to which typical assignments include units closed to women or that are otherwise problematic by gender
- gender representation over time in this career
- gender representation by grade in this career area.

This information was derived from conversations with career area managers and other individuals in the services and from the data available to them. Thus, the richness of the information contained within this chapter is a result of the accessibility of the individuals and quality of information available, including whether data, such as training attrition data, are kept by gender. The small numbers of women in newly opened occupations, who may or may not act in the same way as their successors, have in some cases limited this analysis. Thus, this work has only a limited ability to predict future levels of integration in these occupations. Instead, we offer these case studies to increase understanding of the differences across occupations in processes and job characteristics that may affect levels of integration.

ARMY BRIDGE CREWMEMBER (12C)

Background

Reasons for Selection. The Bridge Crewmember (12C) occupation was selected because of the low percentage of women, as of 1998, in both this occupation and in the occupational class of which it is a part (Infantry, Gun Crews, and Seamanship Specialists). Additionally, because it is a part of the Army career management field Combat Engineering, it offers possibly interesting comparisons with the Marine Corps engineering occupation also selected for analysis in this study.

Occupational Description. The official occupation description states that

> Bridge crewmembers command, serve, or assist as a member of a squad, section or platoon. They provide conventional and powered bridge and rafting support for wet and dry gap crossing operations. (Army, 1999b, p. 21)

Duties for MOS 12C at each level of skill are as follows:

- **E-1 to E-4:** Operates bridge truck and light vehicles. Operates the bridge erection boat. Prepares bridge site, handles shorelines, and assists in rafting operation. Assists in the installation of overhead anchorage system components. Installs kedge anchorage systems. Launches or retrieves ribbon bridge bays. Assists in the assembly of military bridges. Prepares and installs demolition firing systems. Arms, installs, and disarms antipersonnel and antitank mines.

- **E-5:** Directs construction of fighting positions and wire entanglements. Employs the M180 demolition cratering charge. Determines limiting slopes, curves, stream velocities, and gap width. Conducts engineer reconnaissance. Directs crew in the assembly and maintenance of fixed bridges. Directs crew in the assembly of raft and float bridges. Operates and/or supervises the use of bridge erection boats.

- **E-6:** Supervises personnel in the installation and removal of a hasty protective minefield. Collects data and calculates the demolition requirement for explosives and related materials. Conducts road, tunnel, ford, and bridge reconnaissance. Directs the offloading and assembly of float and fixed bridges. Performs float and fixed bridge site layout. Supervises installation of overhead cable anchorage system.

- **E-7:** Assigns tasks to subordinate personnel. Enforces safety standards, field sanitation, communication procedures, security, and job specification. Plans and supervises personnel in the construction of float and fixed bridges. Supervises in mine warfare, demolitions, and combat construction operations. Conducts platoon reconnaissance missions (Army, 1999b, p. 210).

The Circumstances of Opening This Occupation. Women initially entered the Bridge Crewmember occupation in 1995, as they entered the Army and volunteered for this occupation.

How Individuals Access

Individuals join this occupation as they initially enter the Army. Prerequisites include a normal physical profile (vision-correcting glasses permitted), normal color vision, a minimum score of 90 in the combat operations aptitude test, and a valid state motor vehicle operator license. Although not considered part of the physical requirements, the occupational description states that this occupation has a physical-demands rating of "very heavy."

Table 3.2 indicates the numbers of nonprior service accessions that began skill training for the Combat Engineer occupation. The program numbers, or goals, for female accessions have varied considerably, from 62 in 1996 to only 7 in 1998, and back up to 104 in 2000.

Table 3.2

Gender Representation Among Bridge Crewmember Accessions

Fiscal Year	12C Accession Targets				Actual 12C Accessions				% Army Enlisted Accessions Female
	Number			% Female	Number			% Female	
	Men	Women	Total		Men	Women	Total		
1995[a]	118	10	128	7.8	105	6	111	5.4	18.9
1996[b]	383	62	445	13.9	246	40	286	14.0	20.3
1997[b]	127	43	170	25.3	73	17	90	18.9	20.4
1998[b]	20	7	27	25.9	17	7	24	29.2	18.9
1999[b]	154	51	205	24.9	162	41	203	20.2	20.0
2000[b]	175	108	283	38.6	202	104	306	34.0	21.2

SOURCES: Accession numbers for 12C provided by Army PERSCOM. Overall service accession numbers provided by Army DAPE, HQDA.
[a]Data include 15 nonprior service males who entered without needing skill training.
[b]Data indicate only the program and accessions of nonprior service individuals who require skill training.

The proportion of overall accession goals that is female has also varied, from an initial 7.8 percent to approximately 25 percent from 1997 to 1999, to 38 percent in 2000.[1]

Occupational Training Requirements

Combat Engineer training is conducted as One Station Unit Training (OSUT), meaning that new recruits receive their basic training and their skill training in the same unit. This complicates analysis of graduation rates from skill training somewhat, because it is difficult to ascertain whether women are attriting from combat engineer training at a rate higher than that of their male peers or whether they are attriting from the program because of the basic training portion of the course. Table 3.3 addresses this issue by providing the input into OSUT by gender and by deleting estimated attrition from the basic training portion of OSUT, based on the Army basic training attrition rate during that same period.[2] The table then provides the estimated number that would have entered the 12C skill training and the number that actually graduated from 12C training. The final column indicates the adjusted graduation rate from 12C skill training, given the estimated trainees who might have had difficulty with the basic training portion of OSUT.

For example, of the 163 males who entered 12C OSUT in FY 1999, 139 graduated. This results in an OSUT graduation rate of 85 percent. However, during that same period, the graduation rate from Army basic training was 91.1 percent. Thus, the next column estimates the number that would have entered 12C skill training given a 91.1-percent graduation rate from basic training. Given this modeling, the adjusted graduation rate for 12C skill training is 93.6 percent, suggesting that more individuals had difficulty with the basic training portion of OSUT than the 12C skill training elements. This is

---

[1]The Army models used to determine the overall number of accessions desired for each occupation and the proportion of the accessions that should be female have been evaluated in concurrent research being conducted in RAND's Arroyo Center. That research suggests that some of the model assumptions, inputs, and calculations, which eventually limit the number of female accessions, may require adjustment.

[2]This assumes that OSUT trainees will incur the same attrition from the basic training portion of OSUT as do their same-sex peers in the same year.

Table 3.3

Training Graduation Rates Among Bridge Crewmembers

Fiscal Year	Basic Training				12C Skill Training					
	Number Enrolled		Graduation Rate		Estimated Number Enrolled		Number Graduating		Adjusted Graduation Rate	
	Men	Women	Men	Women	Men	Women	Men	Women	Men	Women
1999	163	40	91.1	83.3	148	33	139	27	93.6	81.1
2000	133	53	93.2	87.6	124	46	118	36	95.2	77.6
2001	85	57	93.2	88.9	79	40	77	40	97.1	79.0

especially meaningful for comparison by gender, because female
trainees tend to drop out of basic training at higher rates. Nonetheless, Table 3.3 indicates that even estimating losses from the basic
training portion of OSUT does not completely compensate for
greater female attrition; the adjusted graduation rates range from
93.6 to 97.1 percent among the male trainees, and 77.6 to 81.1 percent among the women. Thus, female trainees likely had greater difficulty with the 12C skill training than did their male peers.

Occupation Assignment Patterns

With the exception of instructor billets at Fort Leonard Wood,
Missouri, and a very small number of other billets, combat engineers
spend their time rotating between Fort Hood, Texas; Fort Polk,
Louisiana; Korea; and Germany. All 12C assignments are open to
either male or female combat engineers, and thus there are no career
restrictions based on limited assignments for women.

Gender Representation

Table 3.4 indicates that the number of female bridge crewmembers
has been steadily increasing since the advent of integration in 1995;
the current representation level is 16.5 percent female. Table 3.5
suggests that women are moving upward through the ranks; the
population currently includes eight female noncommissioned officers (NCOs), and the first bridge crewmembers entered the occupation in FYs 1995 and 1996 (as shown in Table 3.4).[3]

Retention Among Bridge Crewmembers

Table 3.6 indicates the rate of first-term reenlistments among combat engineers. The male combat engineers show a relatively high
reenlistment tendency; from 1998 through 2000, between 61 and 80
percent of them reenlisted into their MOS, and at least 75 percent

---

[3]Note that Table 3.5 and several later tables include data from the Individuals
Account. This account includes students, trainees, transients, hospital patients, and
others. These tables therefore include individuals who may not actually be assigned to
the occupation because they are currently in school, hospitalized, between assignments, etc.

Table 3.4

Gender Representation Among Bridge Crewmembers

| Year | Number in Occupation 12C | | | % |
	Men	Women	Total	Female
1995	770	7	777	0.90
1996	858	37	895	4.13
1997	789	46	835	5.51
1998	657	56	713	7.85
1999	649	68	717	9.48
2000[a]	750	138	888	15.54
2001[b]	747	148	895	16.53

SOURCES: First quarter 1999 Perstempo file; 2000 and 2001 data from Army.

[a]Data as of September 2000.

[b]Data as of March 2001.

Table 3.5

Representation Among Bridge Crewmembers, by Grade

| Pay Grade | Number in Occupation | | | % Female |
	Men	Women	Total	
E-1	40	26	66	39.40
E-2	118	46	164	28.00
E-3	152	56	208	26.90
E-4	129	12	141	8.50
E-5	128	7	135	5.20
E-6	114	1	115	0.87
E-7	66	0	66	0.00
Total	747	148	895	16.53

SOURCE: Combat Engineer Proponency Office.

NOTES: All data are as of March 2001 and include Individuals Account.

overall reenlisted to remain in the Army. Only a small number of women (12 total) have become eligible for reenlistment over the past four years. The majority of these 12 women have reenlisted to remain bridge crewmembers, with only one eligible for reenlistment choosing to leave the Army. Additionally, only two women have become eligible for midcareer reenlistment (one in 1999 and one in

2000), and both reenlisted within 12C. These numbers suggest that representation in this career will continue to increase, as long as the accession targets are held steady or increased.

Observations

This occupation was selected based on our initial analysis of 1998 data, which indicated low female representation. In the past several years, however, the representation of women among bridge crewmembers has continued to increase. This increase results both from accessions (both an increased number of women and an increased share of accessions) and a positive rate of reenlistment. There are no assignment restrictions for female bridge crewmembers, and there is no quantifiable reason that women should not excel in this occupation. As of March 2001, eight of the 316 NCOs in this occupation were female (2.5 percent), and this number should increase as women gain seniority. The only problem noted in discussions with those who manage this occupation was one of physical strength; this occupation does require significant upper body strength for certain tasks. It was noted that this problem is not gender-specific, because some males entering this occupation also

Table 3.6

**First-Term Reenlistment for
Bridge Crewmembers**

	Number at End of First Term		Number Eligible for Reenlistment		% Eligible Who Reenlist in 12C		% Eligible Who Reenlist in Other MOSs	
Year	Men	Women	Men	Women	Men	Women	Men	Women
1994	238	0	208	0	31.0	—	22.1	—
1995	144	0	126	0	32.5	—	4.8	—
1996	140	0	126	0	33.3	—	1.6	—
1997	80	2	61	1	39.3	100.0	4.9	0.0
1998	98	0	58	0	63.8	—	20.7	—
1999	173	12	93	6	61.3	83.3	15.1	16.7
2000	73	8	30	2	80.0	50.0	16.7	50.0
2001[a]	15	4	11	3	45.5	66.7	9.1	0.0

SOURCES: Army DCSPER 628 report; 1998 data modified by Combat Engineer Proponency to remedy missing data.

[a]Data as of April 2001.

have difficulty with some heavy tasks, but that female bridge crewmembers are more likely to have difficulty with some heavy tasks. Nonetheless, female representation in this occupation is now higher than among overall Army enlisted personnel.

ARMY FIELD ARTILLERY SURVEYOR (82C)

Background

Reasons for Selection. The Army Field Artillery Surveyor (82C) occupation was selected for several reasons. First, the inventory data indicate low representation in this enlisted career but high representation in the occupational class, Other Technical and Allied Specialists, in which it is included. Second, artillery careers are problematic in the Army because, while this particular occupation and some officer field artillery opportunities are available to women, many of the units with field artillery assignments are closed to women. Thus, we knew anecdotally that this occupation was problematic for integration.

Occupational Description. The Army has a Web site that lists all enlisted occupations and their job descriptions. The page for this occupation at Army (2000) says that "The field artillery surveyor leads, supervises, or serves as a member in field artillery survey operations." Professionals within the branch explained that the field artillery surveyor surveys the physical location on the ground and establishes a line of known direction to direct artillery fire. According to Army (2000), the tasks involved in this occupation, at the different levels of seniority include

- Entry Level

    — records field data, prepares schematic sketches, and marks survey station

    — performs astronomic observations; measures azimuths and angles, and determines deviations for target, connection, and position area surveys with angular measuring equipment

    — assists the Positional Azimuth Determining System (PADS) operator transfer, strap down, and prepare for operations of PADS

- — computes data using logarithms or calculator to obtain the unknown required field data, including computing for accuracy ratios and adjustment
- — operates and performs preventive maintenance checks and services on vehicles, radios, weapons, and all survey equipment.

- Skill Level Two
  - — supervises and coordinates PADS vehicle operations
  - — computes survey data, plots geographic/Universal Transmeridian grid coordinates and performs azimuth transfer with PADS
  - — operates PADS system; performs calibrations, zero velocity updates, and preventive maintenance checks and services on the PADS system
  - — assists in the collection, evaluation, and dissemination of survey information
  - — provides leadership and technical guidance to lower-grade personnel.

In the past, this occupation involved triangulation with the use of low-technology survey instruments or celestial location and was heavily math-oriented. Within the past 15 years, since integration, the occupation has come to depend more on PADS, which is based on the Global Positioning System, and the daily work is somewhat different. The Army is purchasing the even-more-advanced Improved Positional Azimuth Determining System, which should be fielded by 2005. Service personnel believe that this system could have a dramatic effect on the requirement for 82C, in that the system could move the artillery survey capability to the tactical operators and potentially eliminate (or dramatically reduce) the need for 82C. This recognition is consistent with Army plans to phase out this occupation.

The Army "jobs and skills" site stresses the civilian transferability of field artillery when it describes Career Management Field 13 (CMF 13) as follows:

Field artillery work is highly specialized. On the civilian side, the skills and knowledge acquired in the Army might be translated into meaningful work in a variety of engineering, manufacturing, and production fields. (Army, 2002.)

In summary, this occupation would appeal to someone with strong math skills who was interested in working with a small team in a field environment. The transferability of these skills makes this occupation attractive to such individuals regardless of whether they plan to stay in the Army. It is worth noting that seven of the nine occupations in this career management field are closed to women, so 82C is one of very few opportunities for women who are interested in developing this skill set in the Army.[4]

The Circumstances of Opening This Occupation. This occupation opened as a result of Army policy changes reflecting guidance from the Secretary of Defense. Junior enlisted women began to flow through this occupation in 1994. There is an informal sense, conveyed through personal communications with individuals involved in the field artillery career field, that this occupation was not appropriate for gender integration. No individual interviewed in the context of this research expressed any concerns about female service member's ability to perform the work involved for 82C. Instead, these concerns centered on the assignment problems and thus the limited number of women who could enter this occupation. The official guidance was that women could not be collocated with units whose primary mission was direct ground combat. Because field artillery surveyors are not collocated with these units, the occupation was opened to women. However, field artillery surveyors work in small groups that are often out forward of such combat units, moving to future firing positions. Thus, critics of the decision to open this occupation assert that it places women in greater danger than they would be if they were collocated with some ground combat units.

How Individuals Access

Overall, the occupation recruits fairly well, in some part because it has been integrated; anecdotal reports indicate that the recruiting goals for female recruits fill quickly. Table 3.7 indicates the targets

---

[4]The other field artillery occupation open to women is 93F, which is a low-density (small) MOS that has only approximately 184 authorizations and only about 26 new accessions annually.

and actual accession numbers for 82C. Almost all the female accessions are nonprior service, but 6 to 21 percent of the male accessions in the years examined came from other sources, such as prior service or in service in another MOS. The percentages of 82C accessions that are female vary considerably for two reasons. First, the targets for female accessions vary each year (ranging from 53 in 1996 to only 11 in 1998 and 15 in 2001). The percentage of accession targets allocated for women also varied (19.3 percent in 1996, 5.3 percent in 1998, and 7.4 percent in 2001). These targets stem from the Army accession and recruiting tools, the input for which is based on force structure changes and the current female inventory in the occupation. Second, the degree to which the target for female accessions is met (or even surpassed) also varies considerably year to year.

At the time of this research, the official Army recruiting database, which provides information to potential recruits via Army Web sites, erroneously labeled this occupation as closed to women. It is unclear whether this misinformation may have deterred young women potentially interested in this career field, since female accessions fell 50-percent short of the target for 2000 but fell short by only one individual in 2001.

Occupational Training Requirements

The training program for field artillery surveyors lasts 50 days and focuses upon key skills, such as tactical communications; map reading; determining the distance between stations by mechanical and electronic means; determining direction by astronomic observation and gyroscopic means; operating angular measuring instruments and automated survey systems; recording field data, preparing schematic sketches of field surveys; and computing direction, distance, grid coordinates, height and astronomic azimuth from field data. As Table 3.8 indicates, the majority of female students graduate, albeit at generally lower rates than their male peers. Although the causes for nongraduation are not highlighted below, the proponency office personnel believe that most of the attrition from occupational training for 82C results from academic difficulties.

Table 3.7

Gender Representation Among Field Artillery Surveyor Accessions

| Fiscal Year | 82C Accession Targets | | | Actual 82C Accessions | | | | % Army Enlisted |
| | Number | | % Female | Number | | | % Female | Accessions Female |
	Men	Women	Total		Men	Women	Total		
1996	221	53	274	19.3	193	51	244	20.9	20.3
1997	195	12	207	5.8	147	6	153	3.9	20.4
1998	198	11	209	5.3	139	20	159	12.6	18.9
1999	195	34	229	14.8	139	30	169	17.8	20.0
2000	195	12	207	5.8	147	6	153	3.9	21.2
2001[a]	188	15	203	7.4	118	14	132	10.6	20.5

SOURCES: Accession numbers provided by 82C Proponency office; Overall Army accession data provided by Army DAPE, HQDA.
[a]Data through March 2001.

Table 3.8

Training Graduation Rates for
Field Artillery Surveyors

Year	Number Enrolled AIT		Graduation Rate	
	Men	Women	Men	Women
1996	191	52	83.2	67.3
1997	219	26	78.5	61.5
1998	142	18	84.5	83.3
1999	135	28	83.0	64.3
2000	126	11	77.0	81.8

SOURCE: Field Artillery Proponency Office.

Occupation Assignment Patterns

As mentioned earlier, this occupation has severe assignment constraints by gender. Women are unable to serve at artillery units
below brigade, and many of the 82C billets are at the battalion level.
Additionally, the billets at the brigade level are disproportionately
senior billets; open only to sergeant and above, which further
reduces the assignments available to women. Table 3.9 indicates the
number of authorized billets, or positions, by grade that are open
only to men and that are not constrained by gender. The table
includes only grades up to E-7, because all 82Cs are converted to 13Z
when they are selected to the grade of E-8. In total, less than one-
third of the assignment opportunities for this occupation are open to
women.

Because the assignment opportunities for women are limited, they
cannot develop the same depth of expertise in this career area that
their male peers can. This relative lack of expertise is not likely to
limit promotion opportunities to E-5 or E-6 but is perceived to affect
women's promotability to E-7 or E-8, as occupation-specific expertise is weighted more heavily in the promotion process.

Gender Representation

This occupation is part of the Other Technical and Allied Specialists
occupational class. This occupational class included 1,992 women of

12,097 total personnel in 1998; thus, women were represented at 16.5 percent, which is higher than their representation in the service overall. Table 3.10 indicates the level of gender representation in this occupation since 1994. The level has held steady at approximately 6 to 7 percent female. Table 3.11 shows that the majority of female field artillery surveyors are junior enlisted soldiers; only eight of 53, or 15 percent, are E-5s.

Table 3.9

**Authorized Positions by Grade and Gender
for Field Artillery Surveyors**

Billet Pay Grade	Open Only to Men		Open to Men or Women		Total Positions
	No.	%	No.	%	
E-1 to E-3	59	72.8	22	27.2	81
E-4	187	81.7	42	18.3	229
E-5	173	72.4	66	27.6	239
E-6	40	49.4	41	50.6	81
E-7	20	34.5	38	65.6	58
Total	479	69.6	209	30.4	688

SOURCE: Field Artillery Proponency Office.
NOTE: All data are as of March 2001.

Table 3.10

**Gender Representation Among
Field Artillery Surveyors**

Year	Number in Occupation 82C			% Female
	Men	Women	Total	
1994	880	37	917	4.0
1995	816	54	870	6.2
1996	878	58	936	6.2
1997	884	64	948	6.8
1998	820	69	889	7.8
1999	756	55	811	6.8
2000	707	46	753	6.1
2001	688	52	740	7.0

SOURCE: Field Artillery Proponency Office.
NOTES: Data from year end, except for 2001, which is as of March 2001, and include Individuals Account.

Table 3.11

Representation Among Field Artillery
Surveyors, by Grade

| Pay | Number in Occupation 82C | | | % |
Grade	Men	Women	Total	Female
E-1 to E-3	211	26	237	11.0
E-4	144	20	164	12.2
E-5	190	8	198	4.0
E-6	85	0	85	0.0
E-7	58	0	58	0.0
Total	688	52	740	7.0

SOURCE: Field Artillery Proponency Office.
NOTES: All data are as of March 2001 and include Individuals Account.

Retention Among Army Field Artillery Surveyors

Although it is not immediately evident from the recruiting materials,
policymakers involved in the management of this occupation stress
that this work is often conducted in onerous field conditions. However, the male soldiers have had relatively high retention rates (of
those eligible for reenlistment) in the most recent years. The retention rate for female soldiers is difficult to discern, given the small
numbers; only 11 women have become eligible for reenlistment, and
only four reenlisted into 82C. Table 3.12 displays the first-term reenlistment rates for 82C.

Observations

Women have very restricted career opportunities in this field: Not
many assignments are available to them, and the ones that are closed
are perceived to be very important to growth in this occupation. The
occupation also has other problems, unrelated to gender integration,
in that its grade structure is not self-supporting. That is, the authorizations (or spaces) associated with 82C include an unsupportable
requirement for E-4s and E-5s, as was evident in the total numbers
for each grade shown in Table 3.9. Because of this grade structure,
which includes 239 authorizations for E-5 but only 81 for E-6, very
few individuals get promoted to the pay grade of E-6. Awareness of

this low promotion opportunity may negatively influence retention of both male and female personnel. Additionally, given the low promotion opportunity overall, combined with the assignment restrictions that preclude women from receiving experience with tactical units in this occupation, there is a general perception that women are not likely to be promoted to E-6.

Career managers interviewed for this research asserted that many within the field believe this occupation should not have been opened to women and that the assignments that are open adhere to the letter, but not the spirit, of the official guidance. The official guidance states that women could not be collocated with units whose primary mission was direct ground combat, and 82C personnel actually serve in front of such units in some cases. The variation in female accession targets suggests that this occupation could have been more integrated, absent the assignment restrictions. If, given the technological advances, this occupation is indeed phased out as planned, the issue of integration in this occupation is potentially irrelevant. If not, the grade structure problems need to be addressed for the benefit of both male and female service members. In this and other occupations with similar restrictions, it would be advisable to counsel new female recruits about the extremely limited opportunities available for them within this career.

Table 3.12

First-Term Reenlistment for Field Artillery Surveyors

Year	Number at End of First Term		Number Eligible for Reenlistment		% Eligible Who Reenlist in 82C		% Eligible Who Reenlist in Other MOSs	
	Men	Women	Men	Women	Men	Women	Men	Women
1994	86	0	74	—	31.1	—	17.6	—
1995	133	0	120	—	51.7	—	7.5	—
1996	110	1	92	1	34.8	100.0	7.6	0.0
1997	90	2	72	1	59.7	0.0	12.5	0.0
1999	122	17	62	9	74.2	33.3	12.9	33.3
2000	62	6	22	0	72.7	—	27.3	—

SOURCE: Field Artillery Proponency Office.
NOTE: Data for 2000 are as of March; data were not available for 1998.

The current decision is to phase out this occupation and convert 82C personnel to MOS 13B and 13M within the next five years. However, both 13B and 13M are closed to women. There are, as yet, no plans for how to address the future of the current female field artillery surveyors, given the cessation of this occupation. Further, it is inappropriate to continue accessing women into 82C because their only options when the conversion occurs will be to retrain for a different occupation or to leave the service.

ARMY AH-64 PILOT (152F)

Background

Reasons for Selection. This occupation was selected because it is the largest of the newly opened warrant officer aviation occupations. Additionally, examining an aviation (albeit rotary-wing) occupation in the Army was perceived to complement examinations of the fixed-wing occupations in the Air Force and Marine Corps. This occupation was also selected to include warrant officers in this effort. Although 152F was initially selected for analysis, this discussion will also include 152H when possible, because 152H pilots fly the newer Apache platform, the Apache Longbow.

Occupational Description. Apache pilots fly daytime or nighttime military air assault missions in support of Army ground troops. The Apache Longbow is an especially high-technology aircraft. The weaponry of the AH-64D includes the Longbow Hellfire missile system, the Hydra 70 Rocket system, and a 30-mm gun. In combination with the other technology onboard, this weaponry permits the Apache to engage 16 separate targets within one minute.

The Circumstances of Opening This Occupation. The Army opened this occupation to women almost immediately after legislative changes permitted women to fly combat aircraft. The Army did not compel female aviators already in the system to change aircraft, but women who completed flight training thereafter were assigned to the Apache platform through the same process as their male peers.

How Individuals Access

Approximately 70 percent of Army warrant officer aviators have previously served as enlisted personnel, either in the Army or in another service. The other 30 percent enter the service through the warrant officer aviation program. Almost all of the current female Apache aviators served as enlisted soldiers before entering the flight program. There are no gender-based accession goals either for the Army aviation program overall or for specific aircraft platforms. Only small numbers of women enter the overall aviation program, as shown in the following discussion of training, and most women eventually fly aircraft other than the Apache.

The prerequisites for the aviation program (which serves other aircraft as well) include the following:

- achieve a score of 90 on the Alternative Flight Aptitude Selection Test (AFAST)[5]
- pass the Class 1A Flight Physical Exam
- possess a security clearance
- be between 18 and 30 years of age as of the beginning of flight training.

The preferred qualifications include two years of college at an accredited institution and a private pilot's certificate.

Occupational Training Requirements

The training process for 152F and 152H includes the following courses:

- Warrant Officer Candidate Course, 6 weeks
- Primary Flight Training, 20 weeks
- Combat Skills Flight Training, 12 weeks (for Apache)

---

[5]The Flight Aptitude Selection Test (FAST) measures the special aptitudes, personality, and background characteristics that are predictive of success in the Army's helicopter flight training program. The AFAST is the latest version. This is not an intelligence test but an aptitude test intended to identify optimal candidates for flight training: individuals with sufficient comprehension of complex processes, an ability to adapt to varying spatial relationships, and rapid thought processes. This minimizes the costs associated with admitting inappropriate applicants. The test consists of 200 questions broken down into seven subtests, each of which has separate directions and time limits: Self-Description, Background Information, Instrument Comprehension, Complex Movements, Helicopter Knowledge, Cyclic Orientation, and Mechanical Functions. See Army (1999a) or Army (1987).

- Warrant Officer Professional Development, 4 weeks.

All individuals attend the Warrant Officer Candidate Course, then primary flight training. After primary flight training, individuals are assigned to specific aircraft platforms according to their performance, their individual preference, and platform availability. Few historical data are available on how platforms have been assigned to individuals and how heavily individual preference weighed in the assignment process. However, data do suggest that women tend to fly aircraft other than the Apache; female representation among all qualified Army aviators (as of January 2001) was 2.54 percent (114 female aviators among 4,496 total aviators) compared to 1.35 percent among Apache aviators. Additionally, female Army flight students graduated at a rate of 3.74 percent (26 women among 695 total students) as of January 2001, but their eventual aircraft assignment has not been determined.

Most training attrition occurs during primary flight training. Occupational proponency personnel report that attrition from combat skills flight training, once individuals are assigned to the Apache, is extremely low. This is consistent with the graduation rates for advanced aircraft training in the Apache aircraft, shown in Table 3.13. The men graduated at an average rate of 96 percent, and only one female trainee failed to graduate in the two years of data available. Additionally, seven women and 126 men trained for 152H in 2000. All the women and 123 (97.6 percent) of the men graduated.

Table 3.13

Training Graduation Rates for Army Apache Aviators

Fiscal	Number Enrolled		Number Graduated		Graduation Rate	
Year	Men	Women	Men	Women	Men	Women
1999	311	8	299	7	96.1	87.5
2000	262	16	251	16	95.8	100.0

SOURCE: Aviation Proponency Office.
NOTE: Seven of the 16 FY 2000 female students are 152H.

Occupation Assignment Patterns

Apache pilots are assigned to 15 attack helicopter battalions, in such units as the 101st Airborne Division (Air Assault) and the 82nd Airborne Division. A typical attack helicopter battalion has 24 helicopters; approximately 40 warrant officer aviators, such as 152F or 152H; and approximately 16 commissioned officer aviators. Training assignments are both at Fort Rucker, Alabama, and in Egypt, training Egyptian aviators. None of the assignments is considered more career-enhancing than the others. Only volunteers are assigned to Egypt, and there are always enough volunteers. None of the assignments is closed to women, although pregnant aviators cannot be assigned outside the continental United States (OCONUS). Because of the small numbers and small percentages of women in this occupation, managing pregnancy has not been an issue.[6] The assignment process tries very hard to accommodate dual-career couples, using such means as delaying permanent change of station orders until both members can be assigned to the same destination or assigning aviators to a location in the continental United States (CONUS), even if they were due to be assigned OCONUS, to collocate dual-career couples. Currently, the dual-career issue is not considered a gender issue, because most aviators in dual-career marriages are male. In general, gender is not perceived to be a difficult assignment issue for this occupation, and the assignments of the current female aviators support the lack of any gender-specific process because they are currently distributed across various CONUS and OCONUS locations.

Gender Representation

This warrant officer occupation is part of the Tactical Operations Officers occupational class. In 1998, this occupational class included only 605 women among a total of 11,330 personnel; thus, women were represented at 5.3 percent. Table 3.14 indicates the level of gender representation in this occupation since 1992. The number of women in this career field has increased from 2 in 1992 to 14 in 2001, but the rate of increase has become relatively stagnant. Table 3.15

---

[6]The Army aviation career managers were the only personnel to raise issues of pregnancy or dual-career service members during this research.

Table 3.14

**Gender Representation Among
Army Apache Aviators**

Fiscal	Number in Occupation			%
Year	Men	Women	Total	Female
1992	875	2	877	0.22
1993	866	2	868	0.23
1994	907	5	912	0.55
1995	832	3	835	0.36
1996	801	6	807	0.74
1997	783	9	792	1.14
1998	846	12	858	1.40
1999	936	16	952	1.68
2001[a]	1,017	14	1,031	1.36

SOURCE: Third quarter 1999 Perstempo file.

[a]Data are from Army personnel, as of January 2001, and combine 152F and 152H, which are broken out in Table 3.15.

Table 3.15

**Representation Among Army Apache
Aviators 152F and 152H, by Grade**

Pay	152F		152H	
Grade	Men	Women	Men	Women
W1	27		30	1
W2	64	9	313	3
CW3	103		297	1
CW4	33		115	
CW5	6		29	
Total	233	9	784	5

SOURCE: Aviation Proponency Office.

NOTE: Data are as of January 2001.

includes current 152F and 152H personnel by gender and grade. Of the 14 female Apache aviators, the most senior female is a CW3. The other women are W1 and W2.

Retention Among AH-64 Pilots

Table 3.16 indicates retention for AH-64 pilots. The table includes the total population at the beginning of the fiscal year, the number of pilots that left within that year, and the resulting retention rate. This calculation indicates the rate at which pilots need to be replaced but does not necessarily reflect individual choice to remain in or leave the occupation, because some portion of the pilots included in the population are serving the flight training commitment and thus would not be eligible to leave. This is especially true of the female aviators, many of whom were satisfying the flight training commitment during the years included in this table. Additional time is necessary to assess whether female aviators who have completed their six years of obligated service remain at the same rate as their male peers. In general, the data indicate that the population does tend to retain at high rates.

Observations

Career managers and trainers report that, once female aviators enter training to fly Apaches, their performance is commensurate with that of their male peers, and they do not face career assignment limita-

Table 3.16

Retention Among Army Apache Aviators

Fiscal Year	In Population		Number Retained		Retention Rate	
	Men	Women	Men	Women	Men	Women
1996	983	5	867	5	88.2	100.0
1997	928	6	835	6	90.0	100.0
1998	926	9	846	9	91.4	100.0
1999	879	10	799	10	90.9	100.0
2000	901	16	829	14	92.0	87.5

SOURCE: Army OPMD, Distribution Division.

NOTE: Numbers represent population on first day of fiscal year and personnel lost before end of fiscal year.

tions once qualified as pilots. However, there are very few female Apache aviators, and it is not clear from the data available whether female aviators would prefer to fly Apaches but do not perform well enough in primary flight school to receive their first choice for aircraft platform or whether they prefer to fly other Army aircraft. Given the current rate of female accessions, this occupation is not destined to become proportionately gender integrated. Additionally, it is also not clear whether women, once past their obligated service, will retain as long as their male peers do. If, when eligible to separate, women choose to leave the service at higher rates than do their male peers, gender representation of this occupation is not likely to increase significantly. However, if women stay at rates similar to or higher than their male peers, the representation in this occupation could increase significantly.

MARINE CORPS COMBAT ENGINEER (1371)

Background

Reasons for Selection. Marine Corps Combat Engineer (MOS 1371) was selected for this analysis because of the low percentage of women both in this occupation and in the occupational class, Infantry, Gun Crews, and Seamanship Specialists, in the Marine Corps. This occupation was also of special interest because of possible parallels with the Army combat engineer occupations selected.

Occupational Description. The Marine Corps describes the duties of this occupation as follows:

> Combat engineers construct, alter, repair, and maintain buildings and structures; lift and move heavy objects and equipment by setting up, bracing, and utilizing rigging devices and equipment; and perform various duties incidental to the use of demolitions in construction projects and destruction of objects. Personnel assigned this MOS are taught carpentry and other construction skills as well as demolitions, specialized demolitions for urban breaching and land mine warfare. (Marine Corps, undated.)

Related civilian occupations are carpenters and riggers. Table 3.17 provides the basic functions, with the supporting tasks, of the Marine Corps Combat Engineer occupation.

Table 3.17

Basic Functions of Marine Combat Engineers

Combat Engineer Function	Example Tasks
Mobility	Runway repair
	Breaching minefields, buildings, or other obstacles
	Engineering reconnaissance
	Building military bridges
Countermobility	Laying minefields
	Creating obstacles
	Destroying bridges
Survivability	Building bunkers
	Improving defensive barriers
General Engineering	Vertical construction of buildings, head walls for culverts, etc.
	Building nonmilitary bridges

How Individuals Access

Most 1371s enter the occupation from basic training, although 1361, Engineer Assistant, also serves as a feeder occupation to 1371. To be eligible for 1371, new recruits must have a minimum Mechanical Maintenance test score of 95.

Table 3.18 displays 1371 accessions by gender. Although female recruits have comprised as much as 4 percent of 1371 accessions (in FY 1999), the accession goal for female 1371s was zeroed for FYs 2000 and 2001, because Marine Corps models indicated that it had reached gender saturation for that occupation, given the current assignment restrictions.

Occupational Training Requirements

The basic Combat Engineer Training Course lasts 30 training days, with activities distributed across the basic functional areas as follows:

- general engineering, 11 days
- mobility, 11 days

Table 3.18

**Gender Representation Among
Combat Engineer Accessions**

| Fiscal Year | Number Accessing into 1371 | | | % Female Accessions into | |
	Men	Women	Total	1371	Enlisted USMC
1996	712	10	722	1.39	7.0
1997	691	11	702	1.57	7.7
1998	673	6	679	0.88	8.0
1999	639	27	666	4.05	7.5
2000	729	0	729	0.00	7.5
2001	677	0	677	0.00	—

SOURCE: USMC FY96–FY01 Recruiting Program Plans.

- countermobility, 6 days

- survivability, 2 days.

During general engineering training, Marines learn construction basics, including wood-frame structure, concrete, and masonry block. During the mobility training, Marines learn minefield breaching, obstacle breaching, and military bridging techniques. The countermobility training is designed to teach obstacle construction techniques, such as emplacing minefields and building log obstacles. Survivability training teaches Marines the basics of building fortifications.

Table 3.19 presents the training data provided to us. Information on training success rates by gender had not previously been compiled because the Marine Corps treated this as a gender-blind process. While such processes are ideally gender-blind, such an approach can, in less ideal circumstances, obscure gender-related problems individuals may experience in the training pipeline. In this instance, the data compiled support anecdotal reports that female Marines do exceedingly well in this training program, with all but one female student completing the training satisfactorily during the past several years. The one female student who dropped the training did so for medical reasons and was likely recycled through training.

Table 3.19

**Gender Representation in
Combat Engineer Training**

	Total Students		Female Students	
Period	Assigned	Dropped	Assigned	Dropped
October 1995– April 1997	1,198	28	21	Unknown
May 1997– July 1998	693	17	Unknown	Unknown
August 1998– September 1998	48	0	1	0
October 1998– September 1999	824	36	16	1
October 1999– September 2000	823	8	14	0
October 2000– April 2001	378	13	13	0

SOURCE: USMC.

Occupation Assignment Patterns

Marine Combat Engineers might be assigned to combat engineering battalions, engineer support battalions, and Marine air wing (MAW) support squadrons. Of the total number of authorizations for combat engineers, 1,100 are in combat engineering battalions, 780 in engineering support battalions, and the remaining 528 in MAW support squadrons.

Combat engineer battalions support ground combat units and conduct the first three functions indicated in Table 3.17: mobility, countermobility, and survivability. Engineering support battalions conduct countermobility, survivability, and general engineering functions, as well as perimeter security. The MAW support squadron performs primarily a general engineering function, focusing on expeditionary airfield construction, runway maintenance and improvement, and perimeter security.

Because of their role supporting direct combat ground units, combat engineer battalions are closed to female Marines. Thus, 46 percent of the possible assignments for combat engineers are closed to women. As always, when some opportunities are closed to women, there are several possible results: If the closed assignments are perceived as unappealing to men, the women may be resented for compelling their male colleagues to be assigned to the less-attractive assignments while the women fill the more-appealing assignments. If, on the other hand, the closed assignments represent a large or important portion of the career field, women will likely be disadvantaged in career development because their expertise lacks that particular component. While no data are available to confirm such an assertion, the large percentage of closed assignments in this occupation suggests that female combat engineers' career progression could be disadvantaged. On the positive side, the general engineering skills gained in units open to women are the skills most transferable to the civilian employment market. This is a positive for female combat engineers who either do not want to remain in the Marine Corps or who are pragmatic about the implications of their limited assignment opportunities.

Gender Representation

This occupation is part of the Infantry, Gun Crews, and Seamanship Specialists occupational class. In 1998, this occupational class included only 115 women out of 4,218 total personnel; thus, women were represented at 2.7 percent. Table 3.20 indicates the level of gender representation among combat engineers since 1992.

Table 3.21 indicates the current representation of combat engineers by grade. There are seven female E-4s, four female E-5s, and no women at higher pay grades. Four years could be sufficient time for these women to have progressed to the pay grade of E-4 if they remained in the Marine Corps. These data suggest that women are either not being promoted or are exiting the occupation or the service regardless of promotion opportunities.[7]

---

[7]According to information supplied by Marine Corps personnel, there were 23 women with the 1371 MOS in June 1996. Of these, 17 left the Marine Corps at the end of their contracts, one moved to a different occupation, one is still on active duty, and four were non–end-of-service losses. Some of the women who left at the end of their service were E-4s (Source: Marine Corps).

Table 3.20

Gender Representation Among Combat Engineers

| Fiscal | Number in Occupation 1371 | | | % |
Year	Men	Women	Total	Female
1992	2,540	0	2,540	0.00
1993	2,495	0	2,495	0.00
1994	2,633	1	2,634	0.04
1995	2,626	8	2,634	0.30
1996	2,430	23	2,453	0.94
1997	2,269	26	2,295	1.13
1998	2,181	33	2,214	1.49
1999	2,299	32	2,331	1.37
2001[a]	2,611	34	2,645	1.30

SOURCE: Third quarter 1999 Perstempo file; 2001 numbers provided by Marine Corps.
[a]Data as of February 2001.

Table 3.21

Representation Among Combat Engineers, by Grade

| Pay | Number in Occupation 1371 | | | % |
Grade	Men	Women	Total	Female
E-2	741	0	741	0.0
E-3	607	23	630	3.7
E-4	517	7	524	1.3
E-5	371	4	375	1.1
E-6	170	0	170	0.0
E-7	137	0	137	0.0
E-8	50	0	50	0.0
E-9	18	0	18	0.0
Total	2,611	34	2,645	1.3

SOURCE: USMC-provided data.
NOTES: All data are as of February 2001 and include Individuals Account.

Retention Among Marine Corps Combat Engineers

Retention among combat engineers, as indicated by the first-term reenlistment rates in Table 3.22, is low. Male combat engineers are only reenlisting at rates between 15 and 23 percent. The first four female combat engineers (in FYs 1997 and 1998) did not reenlist. Since then, three out of 26 female combat engineers have reenlisted, producing reenlistment rates of 7.69 percent (in FY 1999) and 15.38 percent (in FY 2000). These rates are problematic because of the small numbers of women involved. However, given the low male reenlistment rates, the female rates would not have to increase much to be on a par with those of their male peers. Additional data available indicate that male combat engineers eligible for intermediate reenlistment choose to remain combat engineers at a rate of about 54 percent, which represents the rate at which those who have become eligible over the past five years have reenlisted. More time will be needed to observe the intermediate reenlistment patterns among female combat engineers.

Observations

The status of gender integration among Marine Corps Combat Engineers is not a simple story. There is only a low level of gender representation, in part because of small numbers of female accessions and

Table 3.22

**First-Term Reenlistment for
Combat Engineers**

Fiscal Year	Number Eligible for Reenlistment		Number Who Reenlist		Reenlistment Rate	
	Men	Women	Men	Women	Men	Women
1995	439	0	66	0	15.03	—
1996	612	0	89	0	14.54	—
1997	584	1	86	0	14.73	0.00
1998	644	3	110	0	17.08	0.00
1999	561	13	128	1	22.82	7.69
2000[a]	509	13	98	2	19.25	15.38

SOURCE: Field Artillery Proponency Office.
[a]Data as of March 2000.

in part because few women have accessed and in part because few female combat engineers have stayed in the occupation. Despite the few women in the occupation, the Marine Corps asserts that this occupation is female-saturated because assignment restrictions preclude women from assignments in 46 percent of the combat engineer billets. As a result of this assertion, the Marine Corps zeroed its accession targets for incoming female combat engineers in FYs 2000 and 2001. Some women still proceed through training, but these numbers are relatively small. Of the women who do attend training, almost all do very well. Indeed, despite the very physical nature of this occupation, Marine Corps personnel interviewed for this research perceived women as performing well in the assignments for which they are eligible. Regardless of their performance, women are likely disadvantaged from progressing to higher pay grades because of the limited experience they can gain in this occupation, but most women leave the occupation or service (with valuable engineering and construction skills) before they would be eligible for promotion to higher ranks. Further analysis of the Marine Corps modeling is warranted to evaluate whether 1.5-percent gender representation (due to assignment restrictions of 46 percent) is a sound management premise. If, on the other hand, the modeling assumptions and calculations are sound, then gender integration in this occupation has reached the goal established.

MARINE CORPS AIR SUPPORT OPERATIONS OPERATOR (7242)

Background

Reasons for Selection. Air Support Operations Operators (7242) were included in this study because of the high gender representation: 1998 data indicate that 17.7 percent of 164 individuals in the occupation were female. This Marine Corps occupation is part of the Communications and Intelligence Specialists occupational class, in which women are slightly more represented overall (7.1 percent, or 643 of 9,072 individuals) as of 1998.

Occupational Description. According to Marine Corps guidelines (Marine Corps, undated a),

> Air support operations operators perform duties incidental to the operation of tactical air support systems, operating various elec-

tronics equipment in a clear and electronics countermeasures environment, performing liaison necessary to ensure effective air support operations, and supervising and participating in preparation, movement, and emplacement of air support equipment.

Another way to describe this occupation is that these individuals maintain an understanding of the ongoing status of aircraft assets available to support ground troops. This occupation directs the air support center and provides an interface between air combat and ground combatants. They are often collocated with the infantry regiment but are not as far forward as the infantry battalions.

According to the USMC MOS manual, those in the 7242 occupation perform the following duties; note that the list also indicates the additional responsibilities the individual incurs with increasing seniority:

- private to master gunnery sergeant:
  - sends, receives, and relays information, requests, and instructions over communication nets
  - implements the principles for operation of air support systems, including the coordination required between air support and other command and control units
  - emplaces, adjusts, operates, and performs first-echelon maintenance on air support electronic equipment, shelters, status boards, plotting boards, and associated equipment
  - plots and converts polar and X-Y coordinates and the various grid systems
  - records data on required status and plotting boards
  - uses correct plotting symbols, radiotelephone procedures, and air command and control terminology
  - maintains operation logs
- corporal to master gunnery sergeant:
  - uses standard emergency procedures when required
  - uses performance characteristics of military aircraft as required

- sergeant to master gunnery sergeant:

  — recognizes various types of interference encountered on electronic equipment and recommends corrective action

  — prepares operations maps and overlays

- staff sergeant to master gunnery sergeant:

  — implements procedures for calibration, orientation, and synchronization of air support electronics equipment

  — implements the principles of the tactical employment of air support units

- master sergeant and master gunnery sergeant:

  — supervises the conduct of operations of the Direct Air Support Center

  — supervises first-echelon maintenance of the equipment assigned to the Direct Air Support Center

  — supervises and participates in the preparation for movement and combat of equipment assigned to the Direct Air Support Center

  — selects positions for and supervises the emplacement of the Direct Air Support Center

- master gunnery sergeant:

  — supervises the conduct of operations of the air support unit

  — coordinates the operations of the air support unit with adjacent air control and antiair warfare units

  — directs and supervises the training of air support personnel.

Air Support Operations Operators serve in an air support squadron, which is part of an MAW. However, the Marine Corps professionals who manage this occupation contrast the experience of this particular occupation with the others the wing comprises. The air support squadrons are the most frequently deployed type of squadron because they are involved in every exercise. The high operations and personnel tempos are believed to be difficult for service members with families or academic aspirations. Additionally, the living conditions for those assigned to the air support squadron tend to be much less comfortable than those for the rest of the MAW. One Marine professional described the Marine air support squadron as the only part of the wing that lives like "grunts," dependent upon what they can carry on their backs or load into small vehicles. These living conditions are perceived to be a surprise to many service members in the 7242 occupation. Nonetheless, the managers of this occupation perceive the women in it to perform exceedingly well.

There are no comparable civilian occupations. The Marine Corps materials cite the Tactical Air Defense Controller occupation, MOS 7236, as a related military skill.[8]

The Circumstances of Opening This Occupation. This occupation was opened to women as a result of the change from the "Risk Rule" to the direct ground combat restriction. Junior female Marines began to flow voluntarily into this occupation in 1995.

How Individuals Access

New recruits enter directly into occupation 7242. The requirements and prerequisites include an ASVAB General Technical score of 100 or higher, normal color vision, U.S. citizenship, and a secret security clearance.

The level of gender representation among nonprior service accessions is indicated in Table 3.23. The number of women accessions into 7242 has decreased, consistent with the Marine Corps models reducing the target for female accessions, given relatively high levels of integration in the occupation.

Occupational Training Requirements

Air support operators must successfully complete the Air Support Operations Operator course, a six-week training program. Table 3.24 indicates the number of male and female marines who enrolled in, and dropped from, the training course in the past three years.

---

[8]Tactical Air Defense Controller (7236) is open to women and includes fewer than 100 individuals. In 1998 and 1999, there were five and eight women in this occupation, respectively, for representation levels of 5.9 and 8 percent (first quarter Perstempo data).

Table 3.23

**Gender Representation Among
Air Support Operator Accessions**

| Fiscal Year | Number Accessing into 7242 | | | % Female Accessions into | |
	Men	Women	Total	7242	Enlisted USMC
1996	49	10	59	16.95	7.0
1997	58	11	69	15.94	7.7
1998	57	5	62	8.06	8.0
1999	57	4	61	6.56	7.5
2000	49	4	53	7.55	7.5
2001[a]	66	4	70	5.71	

SOURCES: USMC FY96–FY01 Recruiting Program Plans.
[a]Data as of April 2001.

Table 3.24

**Training Graduation Rates for
Air Support Operators**

| Fiscal Year | Number Enrolled | | Number Dropped | | Graduation Rate | |
	Men	Women	Men	Women	Men	Women
1998	58	9	5	0	91.37	100
1999	61	5	7	2	88.52	60
2000	61	5	11	1	81.97	80

SOURCE: USMC.

Female attrition has ranged from zero to two individuals, but because of the small numbers of women entering the program, the resulting graduation rate for female Marines in the air support–training program has ranged from 60 to 100 percent. These numbers are higher than the accessions because they sometimes include reservists, or non–entry-level Marines (lateral movers).

Occupation Assignment Patterns

All Marine air support squadrons are open to women. However, the MAW sends a detachment of about 30 people to Marine Expeditionary Units (MEU). A disproportionately large number of those sent, eight, come from the Marine air support squadron. The Marine

Corps has been including female Marines in these MEU detachments since the mid-1990s, with the general policy that, if the MEU ships are configured for women, women may serve on the MEU detachment. However, more-recent interpretation of the DoD guidance for gender integration has questioned this Marine Corps assignment practice. A memorandum from the Marine Corps Deputy Commandant for Aviation to the Marine Corps Deputy Commandant for Manpower and Reserve Affairs (USMC, 2000) explained that the DoD guidance that precludes women from being assigned to units below the brigade level whose primary mission is to engage in direct ground combat conflicts with the Marine Corps practice of assigning women to MEU detachments. The memorandum asserted that this restriction should be removed, because it has

> detrimental effects on the morale, professional development and satisfaction of these Marines while having the simultaneous impact of increasing personnel tempo for their male counterparts. ....
> Additionally, the assignment of females to Air Support Liaison Teams at the Regimental level is both fundamental to the professional development of the individual and an operational necessity. The current policy appears overly restrictive when compared to the DoD guidance and should be reevaluated. (USMC, 2000.)

The Marine Corps has recognized not only that women will lack the opportunities to develop fully their occupational skills and credibility (Marine Corps Deputy Commandant for Aviation, 2000) but also that the male Marines in this occupation will bear an unreasonable burden (and possibly resent their female colleagues) if this policy is not reversed. If the policy is not reversed in this instance and if the Marine Corps ceases to assign women to the MEU detachments, both unit morale and occupational opportunities for women could likely be undermined.

Gender Representation

This occupation is part of the Communications and Intelligence Specialists occupational class, which has a higher level of gender representation as a class (7.1 percent, or 643 of 9,072 individuals as of 1998) than does the Marine Corps overall. Likewise, gender representation among Air Support Operations Operators is also high compared to Marine Corps enlisted representation (6 percent). Table

3.25 shows the representation among 7242 personnel historically, and Table 3.26 indicates the current representation by grade. Although women have not yet progressed to the more-senior NCO ranks, the data indicate that female Marines are remaining in this occupation long enough to be promoted to E-5.

Table 3.25

Gender Representation Among Air Support Operators

| Year | Number in Occupation 7242 | | | % |
	Men	Women	Total	Female
1992	200	0	200	0.00
1993	172	0	172	0.00
1994	179	0	179	0.00
1995	187	9	196	4.59
1996	177	17	194	8.76
1997	139	28	167	16.77
1998	154	28	182	15.38
1999	193	29	222	13.06
2001[a]	219	27	246	11.00

SOURCE: Third quarter 1999 Perstempo file; 2001 data from Marine Corps.

[a]Data as of March 2001.

Table 3.26

Representation Among Air Support Operators, by Grade

| Pay Grade | Number in Occupation 7242 | | | % Female |
	Men	Women	Total	
E-1 to E-3	79	8	87	9.2
E-4	45	9	54	16.7
E-5	36	10	46	21.7
E-6	28	0	28	0.0
E-7	24	0	24	0.0
E-8	6	0	6	0.0
E-9	1	0	1	0.0
Total	219	27	246	11.0

SOURCE: USMC-provided data.

NOTES: All data are as of March 2001 and include Individuals Account.

Retention Among Air Support Operations Operators

The retention data for Air Support Operations Operators indicate some interesting patterns (see Table 3.27). First, the number of men eligible for reenlistment was also relatively small because this is not a large occupation. Second, although none of the female Marines in this occupation reenlisted in FY 1998, which was the first year there were female 7242s eligible to reenlist, they did reenlist in small numbers during the following two years but at rates greater than that of their male peers. Additional data also indicate that all six of the women who have become eligible for intermediate reenlistment (two each in FYs 1997, 1998, and 1999) have reenlisted, whereas male intermediate reenlistment for the past five years in this occupation has averaged only 48.9 percent.

Observations

The Air Support Operations occupation appears to be an integration success story. Women have moved into this occupation, and they are retaining at rates that contribute to an increasing population (and increasingly senior population) of female Marines in this field. All career opportunities are available to women in this occupation, and women are succeeding and being promoted to the higher pay grades. This success suggests that the difficult living conditions and physical aspects of the job are not relevant. Although there are only

Table 3.27

First-Term Reenlistment for
Air Support Operators

Fiscal Year	Number Eligible for Reenlistment		Number Who Reenlist		Reenlistment Rate	
	Men	Women	Men	Women	Men	Women
1995	18	0	7	0	38.89	—
1996	31	0	5	0	16.13	—
1997	38	0	4	0	10.53	—
1998	27	5	8	0	29.63	0.0
1999	33	8	8	3	24.24	37.5
2000	28	10	7	3	25.00	30.0

SOURCE: Marine Corps.

27 women in 7242, this occupation is relatively small, so the current representation (11 percent) is greater than the overall percentage of female enlisted Marines. The accession goals have had to be lowered to maintain the number of women at the current level. Assuming valid model decisions about the ideal level of gender integration in this occupation, integration of 7242 is complete.

There is technically an assignment restriction based on the interpretation of the ground combat exclusion that would preclude female 7242s from being assigned to MEU detachments. However, because assignment of women to MEUs was successful before the restriction was recognized, the Marine Corps has recommended that it be waived for this occupation. If that indeed happens, nothing precludes occupational success for female Air Support Operations Operators.

MARINE CORPS F/A-18 PILOTS

Background

Reasons for Selection. The gender integration of fighter aircraft has received considerable media attention since the legislative change that permitted women to fly combat aircraft. The precursor to this analysis noted both the low number of women flying fighter aircraft as well as the long training pipeline (Harrell and Miller, 1997). It takes time, after all, to make a fighter pilot, and it was not reasonable to expect that there would be high rates of female representation soon after the legislative change. Thus, F/A-18 pilots (as well as Air Force F-16 fighter pilots, discussed later) were selected for this analysis, to assess whether gender integration is progressing as might be expected.

Occupational Description. F/A-18 pilots conduct fighter operations, often from Navy aircraft carriers. This is an occupation open to officers only.

The Circumstances of Opening This Occupation. This occupation had been limited both by the legislation that precluded women from flying combat aircraft and also that which kept women from combatant ships, because F/A-18s operate from aircraft carriers. When the legislative and policy changes reversed the restrictions, the first female pilot trainee in the Marine Corps began flight school in January 1994.

How Individuals Access

Most Marine Corps pilots enter the service with an aviation contract, which guarantees them that, if they maintain their physical condition and complete the Basic School (basic officer training) satisfactorily, they will continue on to flight training. A small number of aviation contracts are given to individuals during the course of the Basic School.

Occupational Training Requirements

It takes several years to create an F/A-18 pilot. Although the duration of this training process can vary based on weather and other factors, it lasts approximately 155 weeks, or 2.9 years, including the transit times between different components of the training process.

This process begins at Aviation Preflight Indoctrination (API), which the Navy conducts at Naval Air Station Pensacola, Florida, for both Navy and Marine Corps pilots. API includes academics, rigorous physical training, water survival, and other basic elements of training that all aviation candidates must complete. Primary flight training follows API. After the 23 weeks of primary flight training, individuals complete "dream sheets" to indicate their preference for jet aircraft, propeller aircraft, or helicopters. Based on class rank, individual preference, and aircraft availability, flight students are assigned one of the three broad categories of aircraft. In a typical year, approximately 186 helicopter slots, 108 jet slots, and 28 propeller slots are available. After assignment to one of the aircraft types, individuals have traditionally proceeded to Intermediate, then Advanced, Flight School, which last 24 and 29 weeks, respectively. This training process is currently being revised. Rather than have students fly the T-2 aircraft for intermediate flight school and the T-A4 aircraft for Advanced Flight School, the Marine Corps is changing the process so that students will fly a new aircraft, the T-45, for both. The new T-45 curriculum will last 41 weeks. Near the completion of Advanced Flight School, the flight students once again submit "dream sheets" with their aircraft preferences, and once again a combination of class rank, preference, and availability determines their assignments. Jet students select between the AV-8B, the EA-6B, and the FA-18. At the completion of Advanced Flight School, the new aviators receive their "wings" and proceed to Fleet Replacement Squadron, where they fly the aircraft to which they have been assigned. Although they have received their wings, this squadron is considered part of the training pipeline.

Occupation Assignment Patterns

Assignment restrictions within the Marine Corps center on the direct ground combat definition and assignment rule. This rule does not restrict pilot assignments, and women can thus serve in any airframe assignment. However, as male and female pilots progress through the ranks, they spend less time in the cockpit, as the Marine Corps likes its officers to have a breadth and depth that encompass more than their primary occupational specialty. Given this, all pilots have the opportunity to experience myriad assignments. However, pilots generally prefer a cockpit over nonflying assignments.

One of the nonflying assignments that pilots can receive is as a forward air controller (FAC), serving with an infantry battalion. Women cannot serve as FACs because of the direct ground combat restriction. This restriction should not hinder a female pilot's promotion competitiveness, both because there are other nonflying assignments that female pilots can fill and because not all male pilots serve as FACs. Nonetheless, conversations with Marine Corps personnel suggest that male pilots may be resentful to the degree that they dislike their own FAC assignments. It is important to note that the existence of female F/A-18 pilots will have very little effect upon the number of FAC assignments that any individual receives (or the likelihood of a male pilot receiving an FAC assignment) unless either the number of female pilots or the number of FAC assignments increases significantly.

Gender Representation

Table 3.28 indicates that there is currently only one female F/A-18 pilot in the Marine Corps. For comparison, 14 F/A-18 Navy pilots were female out of a total 938 as of November 2000, for a level of representation of 1.5 percent (Heines, 2000a). Several major factors

Table 3.28

Gender Representation Among
F/A-18 Pilots

Year	Number in Occupation 7523			% Female
	Men	Women	Total	
1992	335	0	335	0
1993	342	0	342	0
1994	374	0	374	0
1995	419	0	419	0
1996	411	0	411	0
1997	404	0	404	0
1998	401	0	401	0
1999	399	1	400	0.25
2000[a]	470	1	471	0.21
2001[b]	466	1	467	0.21

SOURCES: Third quarter 1999 Perstempo file; 2000 and 2001 data from Marine Corps.
[a]Data as of September 2000 .
[b]Data as of March 31, 2001.

may be limiting the rate of gender integration, in both the Marine Corps and the Navy. First, anthropometrics—the degree to which the plane requires a certain physique—limit the number of candidates who can successfully fly this aircraft. This affects men who are larger or smaller than the average, but it disproportionately affects female candidates.[9]

Additionally, recent investigations into the aircraft selection process have indicated that a surprising number of both male and female candidates who satisfied the anthropometric requirements and who had the class grades necessary to select jet aircraft did not do so. Cultural attitudes may apply here; for example, helicopters are less popular in the Air Force than in the Marine Corps. Candidates may also base aircraft selections on perceived civilian transferability. Finally, there is a perception that jet training is more difficult than training for other aircraft. Some candidates may thus choose to be "winged" in another aircraft rather than risk failing jet training.

---

[9]There are various anthropometric concerns. The most basic among a variety of anthropometric concerns is that individuals must have arms and legs long enough to reach aircraft controls yet still be small enough to eject from the aircraft safely.

This is consistent with recent media coverage asserting that the "best and brightest female pilots" in the Navy and the Marine Corps are not selecting jet aircraft (Heines, 2000b). In FY 1999, six of ten female Navy pilots who scored high enough to select jet aircraft and four of five eligible Marine Corps female pilots declined jet training. Among their male peers, 84 (of 263) Navy male pilots and 40 (of 159) Marine Corps pilots of the same quality also declined to pursue jet training. Further investigation involving field research to capture individual motivations and decision processes would be necessary to get a full understanding of the behavior involved.

Retention Among F/A-18 Pilots

Retention, or any difference in whether male or female personnel remain in a career, is not an important issue for F/A-18 pilots, given the lack of women in this occupation. The current commitment for Marine Corps F/A-18 pilots is eight years of service following "winging." For rough planning purposes, this means that any influx of female pilots in this occupation would accumulate for eight years, making it easier to increase the representation levels than it is in many other occupations

Observations

F/A-18 aviators do not appear to be gaining female representation. Once in this career, women face no structural limitations to their performance and only very minor assignment restrictions. However, despite opportunities female pilots have for success, there is only one female F/A-18 pilot. Regardless of the reasons for the current low number, the current low level of integration is problematic for the future, as female pilots will not graduate from "pioneer" status in this occupation until the numbers grow, and women may be deterred from entering if this occupation is perceived as unwelcoming because the number of women is so low. On the other hand, some women may be motivated to be "the first." Regardless, it is difficult either to predict the future behavior of female pilots or to attract greater numbers of women into these careers until the numbers rise.

AIR FORCE F-16 PILOTS

Background

Like Marine Corps F/A-18s, the integration of women among F-16 pilots has also received media attention since the legislative change that permitted women to fly combat aircraft. Thus, F-16 pilots (as well as the Marine Corps F-18 fighter pilots discussed previously) were selected for this analysis to assess whether gender integration is progressing as might be expected, given the long training pipelines.

How Individuals Access

This occupation is open only to officers. Individuals may enter the Air Force with the desire to fly fighter aircraft and may be guaranteed the opportunity to attend flight school. However, until the individual's flight school performance is assessed and until other factors, such as aircraft availability, are considered, no one knows who will be selected to fly F-16s.

Occupational Training Requirements

The training process for Air Force pilots changed in the mid-1990s, about the time that women began flying combat aircraft. Before then, every flight candidate attended Undergraduate Pilot Training and trained in two aircraft, the T-37 and the T-38. Now all flight candidates attend Specialized Undergraduate Pilot Training (SUPT), the first phase of which is aviation academic training. The second phase of SUPT centers on flight training in the T-37 aircraft, after which individuals "track select" to either fighters and bombers, tankers and heavy aircraft, or helicopters. The assignment process considers individual preferences, instructor recommendations, and aircraft availability. The second phase of SUPT varies according to the track. Those who have been selected to fly either fighters or bombers proceed to the next phase of training, in the T-38. Those who will be flying tankers or heavy airlifters train in the T-1, except those who will be flying C-130s, who train in the T-44. Those selected for helicopters proceed to Fort Rucker, Alabama, and train with Army aviators.

The entire SUPT training pipeline for fighter and bomber pilots is approximately one year, of which the last six months is spent training in the T-38.[10] After this final phase of SUPT, aircraft assignment selection occurs. Once again, individual choice, instructor recommendation, and aircraft availability all influence the assignment process.

Pilots selected for fighter training then attend Introduction to Fighter Fundamentals, in which they learn the different types of formations, basic air-to-ground gunnery, and basic air-to-air tactics. This school lasts approximately one month to six weeks. Pilots assigned to F-16s proceed to Luke Air Force Base, Arizona, for approximately 126 days of training. All told, the training pipeline for F-16 pilots takes almost two years and can be further delayed by inclement flying conditions.

Of the entire training pipeline, the most difficult training, defined by the highest attrition, is that in the T-37 aircraft. Table 3.29 indicates the attendance levels and graduation rates for the academic and T-37 phases of SUPT training. Graduation rates for female flight students have decreased slightly in recent years, compared to 1995 through 1997, and are now lower than the rates for their male peers. Nonetheless, approximately 86 percent of all women who enrolled in SUPT training between 1995 and 2000 graduated, which is relatively close to the male graduation rate of 89 percent.

Table 3.29

Active Duty SUPT Graduation Rates

Fiscal Year	Number Enrolled		Number Graduated		Graduation Rate	
	Men	Women	Men	Women	Men	Women
1995	481	25	416	24	86.5	96.0
1996	554	24	461	21	83.2	87.5
1997	700	31	653	31	93.3	100.0
1998	905	56	823	48	90.9	85.7
1999	1,044	59	904	46	86.6	78.0
2000[a]	675	70	616	59	91.3	84.3

SOURCE: U.S. Air Force.

NOTE: Data also include some students in Euro-NATO Joint Jet Pilot Training, which includes both T-37 and T-38.

[a]Data through third quarter 2000.

---

[10]Flight training durations are estimates, assuming acceptable flight conditions.

The difficulty in assessing gender issues in the long training pipeline for Air Force pilots is that there are no data for the various selection points, such as where individuals are assigned to fighter aircraft, so it is unclear whether women are not being selected for the aircraft they prefer or whether they are not volunteering for F-16 or other fighter aircraft.

Occupation Assignment Patterns

All the units including F-16s are open to women. In fact, these units were open to women serving in other capacities before the legislative changes made the cockpit positions open to female service members. The assignment process is described as gender blind. While this means that women are not likely to be discriminated against in the assignment process—i.e., sent to less-appealing units (were there any deemed as such)—it presents other difficulties. Given the small numbers of female pilots, a gender-blind assignment process distributes women in very small numbers across the squadrons. Thus, female pilots tend to lack a female peer group. Additionally, to the extent that there are any gender-related problems, it is difficult to determine whether a problem is related to gender integration or is actually a personality conflict. Unfortunately, the other assignment policy alternatives have disadvantages. If female pilots were assigned in larger numbers to fewer units, most male pilots would serve only with male peers, and the orientation period for gender integration would proceed almost interminably.

Gender Representation

The number of female F-16 pilots has been steadily increasing since the restriction of combat aircraft was lifted. From 1997 to 2001, there was an approximate increase of five female F-16 pilots each fiscal year, although it is not evident what is driving this rate of increase.

The numbers in Table 3.30 include pilots who have received aircraft assignments, in this case F-16, but are still in the training pipeline and thus have not yet been assigned to operational units. For example, three such women were included in the numbers for each

Table 3.30

Gender Representation Among F-16 Pilots

	Number in Occupation			%
Year	Men	Women	Total	Female
1994	1,827	2	1,829	0.11
1995	1,824	1	1,825	0.05
1996	1,858	2	1,860	0.11
1997	1,881	5	1,886	0.27
1998	1,831	10	1,841	0.54
1999	1,720	15	1,735	0.86
2000	1,619	21	1,640	1.28
2001	1,599	21	1,620	1.30

SOURCE: Air Force.

NOTE: Data represent end-of-fiscal year numbers, except for 2001, which is as of March 31, 2001.

of the years 1999, 2000, and 2001. Deleting these numbers from the total would skew the percentage of representation, however, because their male counterparts were also included in the total number of men in the occupation.

Retention Among F-16 Pilots

According to conversations with Air Force personnel, retention of pilots with six to 11 years of active duty service was approximately 45 percent as of FY 2000. Up to October 1999, pilots incurred a commitment of eight years of service upon completion of undergraduate pilot training, so approximately half the pilots included in this snapshot are eligible to leave the service. More recently, pilots have been incurring a ten-year commitment to active duty service, so future analysis will reflect the behavior of pilots with six to 16 years of service. In general, very few pilots leave the flying community before completing their commitments. Thus, the F-16 community is unlikely to lose more than a small number of female pilots before the year 2008. If women do begin to flow through the training pipeline in more significant numbers, the population would accumulate annually with little loss for at least ten years.

Observations

Once in the occupation, there are no assignment barriers for female pilots and no quantifiable reasons to expect female F-16 pilots not to excel to the same degree as their male peers.

However, few women are becoming F-16 pilots. Previous research found that women were very underrepresented in this occupation but that the long training pipeline precluded rapid population change. Nonetheless, there does not seem to be significant change on the horizon for this career. No more than five or six women seem to be moving into the training pipeline for F-16s a year. The analytic difficulty in assessing the lack of change results from the number of "black boxes" in the pipeline, where critical decisions about the career destinations of flight students are made, but for which data do not exist. Understanding, in depth, why gender representation among F-16 pilots remains low would require research that assesses the elements of the training pipeline that lack data. Specifically, such an effort would seek understanding of the roles individual preference, instructor input, and aircraft availability play. A further objective would be to determine whether male and female flight students had similar preferences and whether they were being satisfied at similar rates.

NAVY GUNNER'S MATE (GM)

Background

Reasons for Selection. This occupation was selected for this analysis because our data indicated low gender representation as of 1998: approximately 1.8 percent of a population of approximately 4,400. The Gunner's Mate occupation is part of the Infantry, Gun Crews, and Seamanship Specialists occupational class, which traditionally has relatively high levels of gender representation overall (see Table 2.9) but which includes many occupations that are underrepresented (see Table 2.12).

Occupational Description. According to the recruiting materials for the occupation (Navy, 1999a),

> [g]unner's mates are responsible for the operation and maintenance of guided missile launching systems, gun mounts, and other

ordnance equipment, as well as small arms and magazines. They work with electrical and electronic circuitry; mechanical, hydraulic and pneumatic systems.

These individuals work with the small arms, armories, and major gun systems onboard Navy ships. The duties performed by GMs include (Navy, 1999a):

- operating and maintaining guided missile launching systems, rocket launchers, gun mounts, and other ordnance systems and equipment
- training and supervising crews in the use of all types of ordnance equipment, from large-caliber guns and missile systems to small arms
- stowing, securing, requisitioning, and reclassifying explosives
- operating and maintaining magazine flooding and sprinkling systems
- making mechanical, electrical, and electronic casualty analysis using technical publications, circuit diagrams, and blueprints
- repairing, maintaining, testing, calibrating ordnance equipment
- servicing hydraulic and pneumatic systems
- repairing, maintaining, testing, and calibrating microprocessing equipment
- repairing damaged hydraulic sealing surfaces, mating areas, and threads
- performing mechanical wire connections, including soldering
- operating and maintaining night optical devices
- operating optical scanning and marking devices to label, identify, and report explosives' utilization and expenditure.

Under qualifications and interests, the Navy material (Navy, 1999a) reads as follows:

Gunner's mates should be capable of learning how to use test equipment and applicable hand tools to perform casualty analysis and arrive at solutions for problems in solid state, digital electronics, microprocessor logic, electrical, hydraulic and mechanical equipment. They should be able to do detailed work, perform repetitive tasks and keep accurate records. Due to the sensitive nature of some of the technical duties, the GM rating has special eligibility standards for reliability, integrity and trustworthiness.

The Navy material also describes the working environment of gunner's mates, emphasizing the variety involved in this work and implying the flexibility required for success in this occupation:

> Gunner's mates work in almost every kind of Navy environment: ship, shore, in the United States or overseas. Their work and specialties may involve indoor or outdoor situations, clean or dirty work, deck or shop, and any kind of climate or environment. They work alone or with others, independently or closely supervised. Their work can be both mental and physical.

The Navy recruiting material indicates similar civilian occupations as listed in the Department of Labor's *Dictionary of Occupational Titles*:

- Stock Control Clerk (ammunition)
- Magazine Supervisor (ammunition; explosives)
- Magazine Keeper (clerical)
- Marksmanship Instructor
- Rocket Engine Component Mechanic
- Artillery Maintenance Supervisor (firearms)
- Ordnance Artificer
- Gunsmith
- Gun Synchronizer
- Ordnance Inspector
- Electronics Mechanic
- Missile Facilities Repairer.

While analysis of the gender representation in these civilian occupations would require further research, these appear to be traditionally male occupations, and the percentage representation of women in them is likely low.

The Circumstances of Opening This Occupation. No institutional information is currently available on how integration was initiated, or the exact date that women entered the training pipeline for the gunner's mate rating. These positions existed on ships open to women before the legislative changes. For example, Navy tenders, although they do not have big guns, do have small arms. Navy personnel who manage this occupation surmise that opening the combatant ships to women must have made it worthwhile to open this occupation to women, because only a limited number of positions would have been open to women within this occupation before the legislative changes.

However, our data analysis and discussions with Navy personnel suggested that, when this occupation was opened to women, only female volunteers entered the occupation (no women were compelled to enter) and that these women were junior service members who attended A School with male service members in their accession cohort.

How Individuals Access

Most gunner's mates enter the occupation directly from basic training. A small percentage, estimated at not more than 10 percent of gunner's mates, "strike" (or transfer), into the occupation from other occupations. The required ASVAB formula is as follows:

$$MK + EI + GS + AR = 204 ,$$

where MK is mathematics knowledge, EI is electronic information, GS is general science, and AR is arithmetic reasoning. This is lower than the STG occupation (discussed in the next subsection) accession prerequisite scores for the same ASVAB components. The only other selection restrictions are that gunner's mates must be U.S. citizens eligible for a security clearance and that normal hearing and normal color perception are required (Navy, 1999a).

Gender representation among those joining this occupation is indicated in Table 3.31. These data indicate that gender representation among the gunner's mate rating accessions has ranged from 6.1 to 12.1 percent, while the gender representation of overall Navy accessions has ranged from 14.1 to almost 20 percent. FY 2001 is the first

Table 3.31

**Gender Representation Among
Gunner's Mate Accessions**

Fiscal Year	Number Accessing into GM			% Female Accessions into	
	Men	Women	Total	GM	Enlisted Navy
1994	465	40	505	7.92	16.8
1995	392	28	420	6.67	19.9
1996	341	22	363	6.06	15.0
1997	309	31	340	9.12	14.1
1998	328	45	373	12.06	19.1
1999	592	62	654	9.48	18.1
2000	530	55	585	9.40	18.3

SOURCE: Navy Recruiting Command.

year for which there were accession targets by gender for gunner's mates because this occupation was listed in a second-priority category of underrepresented ratings (less than 10-percent female). The targets were 97 female and 576 male accessions, or 16.8 percent female accessions. Even though the targeted and past actual accession percentages are lower than the overall Navy rates for female accessions, they are still considerably higher than the overall representation in the rating (Table 3.32). The disparity between the representation among accessions and the current population of gunner's mates suggests possibly disproportionate female attrition; attrition is discussed below.

Occupational Training Requirements

The most basic level of occupational training for gunner's mates, A School, lasts 16 weeks. Table 3.33 indicates the enrollment and graduation rates for Gunner's Mate A School. With the exception of FY 2001, for which only partial data were available, women graduate from A School at a higher rate than do men. In general, the graduation rates are relatively high, and individuals from the Naval Gunnery School report that few individuals have academic difficulties.

More-advanced, follow-on training (known as C School) is available for selected individuals. There are five different kinds of C School,

Table 3.32

Gender Representation Among Gunner's Mates

| | Number in Occupation | | | % |
Year	Men	Women	Total	Female
1992	6,757	0	6,757	0.00
1993	6,021	4	6,025	0.07
1994	5,371	7	5,378	0.13
1995	5,268	41	5,309	0.77
1996	5,145	58	5,203	1.11
1997	4,751	73	4,824	1.51
1998	4,405	74	4,479	1.65
1999	4,172	100	4,272	2.34
2000	4,037	183	4,220	4.35

SOURCES: Third quarter 1999 Perstempo file. Navy data for year 2000.

Table 3.33

Gunner's Mate A School Graduate Rates

| Fiscal Year | Number Enrolled | | Number Graduated | | Graduation Rate | |
	Men	Women	Men	Women	Men	Women
1999	493	48	425	43	86.2	89.6
2000	496	55	450	50	90.7	90.9
2001[a]	196	16	176	12	89.8	75.0

SOURCE: Naval Gunnery School.
[a]Data as of April 2001.

each of which focuses on different weapon systems: Vertical Lauch System, Mark 45 (5-inch gun), Mark 75 (76-mm gun), Mark 26 (missile launcher), Mark 13 (missile launcher). Of these weapon systems, the Mark 13 and the Mark 75 are located only on guided missile frigates (FFGs), which are closed to women. As a result, women are assigned only to the other three C Schools.

Occupation Assignment Patterns

Although only certain classes of ships have major gun systems, each ship has an armory. Thus, there are gunner's mates on all Navy ships, although not all Navy ships are open to women. The ships that are closed to women but that do have gunner's mates are generally smaller, such as frigates and patrol craft. Most individuals consulted in the course of this research agree that there is little career enhancement associated with assignment to these smaller ships. Instead, the most highly valued assignment opportunities for gunner's mates are perceived to be those on guided-missile destroyers (DDGs) and cruisers (CGs) because of the advanced major weapon systems onboard. These assignments are open to women. Although we found no policies in place to indicate that women were actively being selected for these assignments, we also found no perceptions among the community managers and detailers that women were excluded from them. Nonetheless, one premise of this research was that there may be unequal assignment practices unless there are proactive policies in place to ensure equality. The small numbers of women at the higher grades in this rating make it especially difficult to evaluate whether women are being assigned equitably.

Gender Representation

This occupation is part of the Infantry, Gun Crews, and Seamanship Specialists occupational class. In 1998, this occupational class included 3,470 women out of 21,053 total personnel; thus, women were represented at 16.5 percent, which is higher than their representation in the overall service. Table 3.32 indicates the level of gender representation among gunner's mates since 1992. Table 3.34 indicates that, despite female representation in this occupation dating to 1993, only one female gunner's mate is an E-7, and only 14 percent of the female gunner's mates are E-5s. This results from the low retention rates described below.

Retention Among Navy Gunner's Mates

Table 3.35 indicates the retention rates of gunner's mates since FY 1993 for the various reenlistment zones (based on years of service). Retention statistics are problematic with such small numbers of women, and was not until the most recent years that sufficient numbers of women were eligible for reenlistment to draw conclusions. Even so, the year-to-year retention rate for women varied considerably from 1996 through 2000, but reenlistment rates were low in

Table 3.34

**Representation Among
Gunner's Mates, by Grade**

Pay	Number in Occupation			%
Grade	Men	Women	Total	Female
E-1 to				
E-3	546	55	601	9.15
E-4	878	101	979	10.32
E-5	1,129	26	1,155	2.25
E-6	884	0	884	0.00
E-7	530	1	531	0.19
E-8	57	0	57	0.00
E-9	13	0	13	0.00
Total	4,037	183	4,220	4.35

SOURCE: Navy.
NOTE: All data are as of December 2000 and include
Individuals Account.

most of these years. Additionally, the data provide some support to
anecdotal reports of low retention rates among women. However,
despite the data indicating that only about one-fourth of the male
gunner's mates reenlisted the first time they were eligible, some Navy
personnel have the perception that almost all women separate at the
first opportunity (without recognizing similar tendencies among
their male peers).

While most male gunner's mates do not stay in, the majority of those
who do reenlist as gunner's mates are likely to remain in the service.
Only five women have made retention decisions beyond their first
reenlistment. Of these, two have remained gunner's mates . Until
women reach higher tenure in greater numbers, it will not be evident
whether more-senior female gunner's mates also retain at higher
rates.

Observations

This occupation involves hands-on work in armaments, an area that
many perceive to be less appealing to women. The civilian equivalent careers described in the recruiting material and the career
description in the recruiting material cast the work as involving both

Table 3.35

Retention Among Navy Gunner's Mates

Years of Service	Fiscal Year	Number Making Retention Decision		% Retained	
		Men	Women	Men	Women
<6	1993	960	0	28.9	—
	1994	936	1	26.5	100.0
	1995	660	4	34.8	0.0
	1996	437	9	31.1	0.0
	1997	665	8	25.5	12.5
	1998	593	39	26.9	17.9
	1999	552	33	28.8	30.3
	2000	463	20	26.8	15.0
6–10	1993	416	0	68.0	—
	1994	406	0	53.4	—
	1995	354	0	62.1	—
	1996	299	0	64.8	—
	1997	281	1	54.8	0.0
	1998	210	0	59.5	—
	1999	205	0	58.5	—
	2000	215	2	63.3	50.0
>10	1993	197	0	76.1	—
	1994	264	0	62.5	—
	1995	232	1	77.1	100.0
	1996	242	0	76.0	—
	1997	261	0	75.5	—
	1998	259	1	74.1	0.0
	1999	237	0	75.5	—
	2000	209	0	78.9	—

NOTE: Data for 1993–1998 combine GMG and GMM ratings, which were subsequently merged into the GM rating.

"clean and dirty" work. Those who manage this career believe that the women who enter the service as gunner's mates leave at their earliest opportunity, despite the fact that most of their male peers do the same. There does not appear to be any systemic discrimination by gender, but there also do not appear to be any policies to investigate or ensure fair treatment. Given the perception that women will leave the occupation, there may even be a tendency to give the more-elite assignments (those on DDGs and CGs) to men. However, with such small numbers, especially at the more-senior ranks, it is difficult to ascertain fairness in policies.

NAVY SONAR TECHNICIAN-SURFACE

Background

Reason for Selection. Although the STG occupation is similar in size to that of gunner's mates (there were 3,995 STGs and 4,402 gunner's mates in 1998), gender representation in this Navy enlisted position is higher than in the gunner's mate occupation. As of 1998, 8.9 percent of the Navy's 3,995 STGs were female.

Occupation Description. Navy (1999b) says that

> These technicians are operators and electronics technicians responsible for keeping sonar systems and equipment in good operating condition on surface ships such as frigates, minesweepers, destroyers, cruisers or at remote locations throughout the world. They are responsible for underwater surveillance, and aid in safe navigation and search-and-rescue operations. They use sonar to detect, analyze and locate targets of interest.

There are two kinds of sonar technician occupations for surface ships: Sonar technicians (STG) are responsible for operating sonar systems and have a four-year service commitment. A Sonar Technician Advanced Electronics Field (STG-AEF) both operates and maintains equipment. Because the latter variation involves additional training, STG-AEF has a six-year service commitment. STGs and STG-AEFs perform the following duties (Navy, 1999b, 1999c):

- identify sounds produced by surface ships, torpedoes, submarines, evasion devices, marine life, and natural phenomena
- operate sonar sensors for detection and classification of contacts
- identify the characteristics, functions, and effects of controlled jamming and evasive devices on sonar operations
- prepare and interpret sonar messages
- operate underwater fire control systems for firing torpedoes and antisubmarine rockets
- recognize major equipment malfunctions during sensor operations
- operate tape recorders, bathythermographs, and fathometers
- operate underwater communications equipment.

STG-AEFs perform the following additional duties:

- operate computer localization subsystems and data entry terminals
- use hand tools and portable power tools
- use and maintain hand tools and portable power
- perform preventive and corrective maintenance on sonar equipment and underwater fire control systems including use of general purpose test equipment
- identify electronic components on schematics and tracing major system flow
- operate underwater communications equipment.

Navy material describing the working environment of STGs emphasizes the positive of the highly technical occupational environment, such as cleanliness, teamwork, and self-supervision (Navy, 1999b, 1999c): "STG/STG-AEFs usually work indoors in clean, shop-like environments and computer equipment rooms. They work closely with others and require little supervision."

Similar Civilian Occupations and Similar Occupations in Other Services. The Navy recruiting material indicates that the following civilian occupations, as listed in the Department of Labor's *Dictionary of Occupational Titles,* are similar to STG:

- Microcomputer Support Specialist
- Technical Support Specialist
- Data Communications Analyst
- Instructor, Technical Training
- Computer Operator
- Electronics Tester
- Electronics Utility Worker.

The occupations listed as similar to STG-AEF, which includes more training and a longer commitment than the basic STG occupation, also include the following:

- Electronics Technician
- Instrumentation Technician
- Computer Security Coordinator
- Computer/Peripheral Equipment Operator
- Fire Control Mechanic
- Office Machine Server
- Electromechanical Technician
- Instrument Repairer
- Repairer, Probe Test Card, semiconductor wafers
- Electronics Inspector
- Electronic Equipment Repair
- Reworker Printed Circuit Board
- Data Communication Technician
- Electronics Mechanic.

These occupations are clearly technical, implying that the recruit will receive valuable, civilian-transferable training. Note that the comparable occupations are very different from those listed for gunner's mates. Note also that determining the gender representation in each of the civilian occupations would require additional research, but the lists above do provide a general sense of the work as it is described to a potential new recruit.

Circumstances of Opening (Law or Policy). There is no institutional memory of the precise decisions or policy changes that opened this occupation, but positions within this occupation exist only on anti-submarine warfare–capable ships. Thus, the occupation likely opened to women at the same time such ships opened to women.

How Individuals Access

Most STGs enter the occupation directly from basic training. The requirements for this occupation include required ASVAB scores as follows:

- MK + EI + GS = 156

- MK + EI + GS + AR = 218

- MK, AR, minimum 57 ,

where MK is mathematics knowledge, EI is electronic information, GS is general science, and AR is arithmetic reasoning. The Navy material (Navy, 1999b, 1999c) also indicates that STGs

> should have excellent hearing, an aptitude for electricity and electronics; skills in arithmetic, speaking and writing; the ability to do detailed work; read and comprehend written instructions; keep records; perform as a team member; curiosity; resourcefulness; a good memory; and manual dexterity with tools, equipment and machines.

U.S. citizenship is also required, for security reasons, and normal hearing, normal speech, and normal color perception are required.

Table 3.36 shows gender representation among STG accessions. The representation rates increased considerably within the first couple of years. Although the percentage of women entering the STG occupation has fluctuated somewhat, it has remained relatively high considering that this career is not a traditional opportunity for women and that the percentage of women accessing into STG in 1999 was higher than among overall Navy accessions. This occupation has consistently had specific goals by gender. The 2001 accession goals for STG were 566 men and 130 women; this translates into a target of 23-percent female accessions for 2001, which is aggressive given the past overall percentage of female accessions into the Navy.

Occupational Training Requirements

The most basic level of training for STGs, A School, lasts ten weeks and is followed by seven weeks of operations courses. The STG operators who entered the service with a four-year commitment then proceed to another four weeks of operational training. They complete a total of 21 weeks of training.

The STG technical operators, who enter the service with six years of commitment, proceed from the various operations courses to nine weeks of digital electronic training. Next is C School training in systems maintenance, which lasts from 17 to 35 weeks, depending on the kind of ship to which the individual will be assigned. By the end of C School, these STGs will have completed 43 to 63 weeks of training.

The A School graduation rates are indicated in Table 3.37. The male graduation rates tend to be slightly higher because the rate of legal and administrative separations is higher among female students.

Table 3.36

Gender Representation Among Sonar Technician Accessions

| Fiscal Year | Number Accessing into STG | | | % Female Accessions into | |
	Men	Women	Total	STG	Enlisted Navy
1994	360	5	365	1.37	16.8
1995	255	26	281	9.25	19.9
1996	332	45	377	11.94	15.0
1997	606	74	680	10.88	14.1
1998	516	109	625	17.44	19.1
1999	401	102	503	20.28	18.1
2000	383	71	454	15.64	18.3

SOURCE: Navy Recruiting Command.

Table 3.37

Sonar Technician A School Graduation Rates

| Fiscal Year | Number Enrolled[a] | | Number Graduated | | Graduation Rate | |
	Men	Women	Men	Women	Men	Women
1997	509	82	411	63	80.7	76.8
1998	580	98	509	67	87.8	68.4
1999[b]	380	88	301	70	79.2	79.5
2000[b]	203	33	171	26	82.2	78.8

SOURCE: U.S. Navy Antisubmarine Warfare Training Center.

[a]Does not include students who left program for officer programs or for BUD/EOD.

[b]Does not include those still in training.

Occupation Assignment Patterns

STGs are assigned to carriers (CVs), CGs, destroyers (DDs), DDGs, and FFGs. Women can be assigned to any STG assignment except for those on FFGs, which are closed to women. Only 280 STG assignments (7 percent of the total) are on FFGs, and FFG assignments are not necessarily considered important for career advancement.

Gender Representation

The STG occupation is part of the Electronic Equipment Repairers occupational class. In 1998, women were underrepresented in this occupational class, because only 7.1 percent of the 14,743 personnel were women. Of the occupations previously open in this occupational class, women remained underrepresented in about half (as of 1998).

Table 3.38 shows that women constituted approximately 10 percent of the STG occupation as of the end of 2000, and this level has been growing consistently since 1993. Table 3.39 indicates that female STGs are also advancing through the ranks, constituting roughly 4 percent of E-6 to E-8 personnel and 10 percent of E-5s.

Table 3.38

Gender Representation Among
Sonar Technicians

| | Number in Occupation STG | | | % |
Year	Men	Women	Total	Female
1992	5,187	0	5,187	0.00
1993	4,439	1	4,440	0.02
1994	3,988	10	3,998	0.25
1995	3,638	26	3,664	0.71
1996	3,355	89	3,444	2.54
1997	3,317	181	3,498	5.17
1998	3,642	349	3,991	8.74
1999	3,637	366	4,003	9.14
2000	3,450	389	3,839	10.13

SOURCES: Third quarter 1999 Perstempo file. Navy data for year 2000.

Table 3.39

Representation Among Sonar
Technicians, by Grade

Pay	Number in Occupation			%
Grade	Men	Women	Total	Female
E-1 to				
E-3	425	74	499	14.83
E-4	763	153	916	16.70
E-5	951	104	1,055	9.86
E-6	821	38	859	4.42
E-7	347	15	362	4.14
E-8	103	5	108	4.63
E-9	40	0	40	0.00
Total	3,450	389	3,839	10.13

SOURCE: Navy.
NOTE: All data are as of December 2000 and include
Individuals Account.

Retention Among Navy Sonar Technicians

The retention data are shown in Table 3.40. The table indicates the
number of individuals, by gender and by years of service, who made
a retention decision and the percentage of those who remained in
the Navy as a sonar technician. For example, in FY 2000, 31.9 percent
of the 423 male STGs who were eligible to make a retention decision
remained in the occupation. Within the last three years of data,
approximately 20 percent of female STGs retained. While not as high
as the male retention rate for first-termers, this rate is contributing to
an increasing number of senior female STGs. Among the more-
senior ranks, the retention rate has fluctuated, but the majority of
female STGs with greater than six years of service chose to remain in
the service in 2000.

Observations

The prerequisites for STGs are designed to ensure that the accessing
personnel, and thus the working population, are intelligent and
capable. Sonar technicians receive highly technical training, which
is perceived to have positive civilian value, and work in a clean, high-

Table 3.40

Retention Among Navy Sonar Technicians

Years of Service	Fiscal Year	Number Making Retention Decision		% Retained	
		Men	Women	Men	Women
<6	1993	847	0	20.7	—
	1994	665	2	15.6	50.0
	1995	422	5	16.1	20.0
	1996	373	6	23.6	50.0
	1997	532	20	34.2	30.0
	1998	476	72	25.5	19.4
	1999	399	59	25.8	20.3
	2000	423	67	31.9	20.9
6–10	1993	284	0	52.8	—
	1994	340	0	39.4	—
	1995	207	1	43.5	100.0
	1996	225	0	43.1	—
	1997	177	4	62.2	75.0
	1998	144	39	62.5	35.9
	1999	95	18	69.5	38.9
	2000	79	14	59.5	64.3
>10	1993	161	0	70.8	—
	1994	210	0	58.1	—
	1995	135	0	72.6	—
	1996	147	0	71.4	—
	1997	148	2	74.3	50.0
	1998	159	18	65.4	44.4
	1999	104	11	70.2	36.4
	2000	80	6	61.3	50.0

technology environment. These factors may all appeal to female accessions, as the percentage of STG accessions has approached or exceeded the percentage of overall Navy female accessions. Once in the occupation, there are few barriers to success for women. Most assignments are available to women; the positions that are closed are not considered more critical to career advancement than other assignments. The women who have entered this career have retained at rates that, while lower than those of their male colleagues, are high enough to develop a more-senior female population of STGs. This occupation does not yet have the same level of gender representation as the Navy enlisted population overall but could approach that level within a couple of years if behavior remains consistent and if STG accessions continue to include 15 to 20 percent female recruits.

NAVY SURFACE WARFARE OFFICER

Background

SWOs serve on all Navy surface ships. Because some SWOs serve on noncombatant ships, this occupational area was open to women before the mid-1990s. Although the rest of this analysis focuses on newly opened occupations, SWOs are included in this research for two reasons. First, the legislative and policy changes that opened combatant ships to women changed the nature of this occupation dramatically for women. Second, because this occupation includes the largest number of female naval officers who have selected non-traditional occupations, any integration issues in this occupation have the potential to have large effects on the careers of female naval officers.

At the time the legislative and policy changes were enacted, a small population of female SWO officers had already been serving on non-combatant surface ships. This group thus became immediately available for assignments to combatant ships. Since then, like their male peers, female SWOs have entered the Navy and had career assignments that included both combatant and noncombatant ships.

How Individuals Access

Officers access into SWO from three main sources: the U.S. Naval Academy at Annapolis, Maryland; Naval ROTC programs and the Enlisted Commissioning Program; and Officer Candidate School. Approximately half of all naval officers are unrestricted line officers. Such officers fill most of what might be called the "warfighting" types of occupations in the Navy. The occupational areas within unre-stricted line are special operations (e.g., explosive ordnance dis-posal), special warfare (SEALs), fleet support, submarines, aviation, and surface warfare. Fleet support, which is oriented toward shore duty, has a disproportionate number of female officers, as a result of earlier policies restricting women from being assigned to combat ships, but accessions to fleet support are currently frozen. Women are precluded from serving in special warfare or submarines; only very small numbers of women enter special operations; and only modest numbers of women enter Navy aviation. Thus, the largest share of women entering the unrestricted line today become SWOs. This is especially true among female graduates of the U.S. Naval Academy because all academy graduates must enter the unrestricted line. Table 3.41 indicates the percentages of surface warfare accessions that were female, from FY 1992 to April 2001.

Surface warfare has an additional appeal for some junior officers: It has the shortest training pipeline and the shortest required commitment of the unrestricted line career opportunities. Thus, this occupational opportunity would have additional appeal to unrestricted line officers who were not initially interested in locking in a career in the Navy. Other officers become SWOs after performing below standard in aviation or nuclear training. Retention patterns are discussed below.

Table 3.41

**Gender Representation Among
Surface Warfare Officer Accessions**

| Fiscal Year | Number Accessing into SWO | | | % Female Accessions into | |
	Men	Women	Total	SWO	Naval Officers
1992	764	26	790	3.3	18.9
1993	640	29	669	4.3	17.3
1994	620	80	700	11.4	15.8
1995	701	99	800	12.4	17.7
1996	686	148	834	17.7	16.1
1997	607	116	723	16.0	17.2
1998	612	129	741	17.4	17.1
1999	649	196	845	23.2	18.2
2000	673	239	912	26.2	18.3
2001[a]	684	266	950	28.0	

SOURCE: Provided by Navy Surface Warfare Community.
[a]Data estimated as of April 2001 and reflect commitments and plans, not actual accessions.

Occupational Training Requirements

SWOs attend Surface Warfare Officer School, Division Officer Course at Newport, Rhode Island, following their commissioning. This four- to six-month training pipeline instructs the new officers in ship driving, basic warfighting skills, shipboard management, and administrative skills. The graduation rates are close to 100 percent, as typically only unmotivated individuals are unable to complete this course.

Following completion of the training course, an officer is assigned to his or her first division officer tour onboard a surface ship. During this tour, the officer learns the capabilities of the ship and its systems and qualifies in a number of key watch stations. Successful completion of these steps leads to surface warfare qualification.

Occupation Assignment Patterns

Almost all surface ships, with the exception of patrol craft, are technically open to women. While ship reconfiguration has generally been necessary for female enlisted personnel to serve on combatant ships, this is considerably less of an issue for female officers, because officer berthing and accommodations are generally more flexible. Thus, as indicated earlier in Table 2.18, female officers do serve on ships that are not available for female enlisted members.

Command opportunity is related to the issue of assignments and is an excellent measure of the career opportunities and success of women in the occupation. In the case of SWOs, this is a good news story for gender integration. Despite the relatively small number of female SWOs in grades O-5 and O-6 (currently 30; see below), female SWOs have a high rate of selection for command. At the time of this writing, two women commanded combatant ships, two served in shore commands, and four female SWOs served as executive officers aboard combatant ships. In addition, eight women were slated to command combatant ships, and two women were slated to serve as executive officers on combatant ships. Five other women had previously commanded combatant ships and seven more have commanded logistics ships, one as a major (Captain) commander.

It is important to note, however, that the "pioneer effect" may have positively influenced the selection for command. Personnel managers believe that individuals who joined this community before the lifting of the combat exclusions have performed and acted differently because they were pioneers. The women who entered, in much larger numbers, after the combat exclusion was lifted will likely not behave in the same ways. The data already indicate that these younger cohorts have no gender difference in selection rates for department head assignments.

There is an assignment issue for SWOs that does have gender consequences, however. The surface warfare career has a preponderance of sea tours. The typical SWO officer will spend the first five years of his or her career at sea, the next two to three years or so ashore, and then the next five years back at sea. For individuals, male or female, who place a priority on spending time with their families, this is problematic. Anecdotal evidence and exit interviews suggest that women who want to have children also find this career path problematic.

Gender Representation

Table 3.42 indicates the number of female officers who had qualified for SWO or were in training for SWO qualification, from 1992 to 2000. These data indicate that gender representation among SWOs is steadily increasing and that representation among junior officers training for surface warfare qualification is disproportionately high. This is consistent with the limited alternative opportunities for female officers interested in or obligated to unrestricted line careers in the Navy.

Table 3.43 indicates representation within the surface warfare community by rank, as of January 2001. The data reflect an increasing number of young female officers entering this community, consistent with the data in Table 3.41.

Retention Among SWOs

As with all occupations that have relatively small numbers of women eligible to separate from the service, retention rates can vary dramatically year to year and can also be misleading simply because of the small numbers. Table 3.44 shows retention data for various year

Table 3.42

Gender Representation Among Surface Warfare Officers

Fiscal Year	Number Qualified			In Training			Total % Female
	Men	Women	% Female	Men	Women	% Female	
1992	8,424	164	1.9	2,804	102	3.5	2.3
1993	7,884	174	2.2	2,329	89	3.7	2.5
1994	6,975	167	2.3	2,108	141	6.3	3.3
1995	6,526	165	2.5	2,150	210	8.9	4.1
1996	6,368	201	3.1	2,033	285	12.3	5.5
1997	6,330	246	3.7	1,850	307	14.2	6.3
1998	6,046	315	5.0	1,716	305	15.1	7.4
1999	5,884	361	5.8	1,619	383	19.1	9.0
2000	5,764	413	6.7	1,807	522	22.4	11.0

SOURCE: Surface Warfare Community.
NOTES: All data for October of the year indicated. "Qualified SWO" includes individuals with 111x designator; "SWO in Training" includes individuals with 116x designator.

Table 3.43

Representation Among Surface Warfare Officers, by Grade

Pay Grade	Number in Occupation			% Female
	Men	Women	Total	
O-1	1,299	433	1,732	25.0
O-2	1,283	231	1,514	15.3
O-3	1,980	201	2,181	9.2
O-4	1,057	19	1,076	1.8
O-5	982	22	1,004	2.2
O-6	508	8	516	1.6
O-7	26	0	26	0.0
O-8	18	0	18	0.0
O-9	8	0	8	0.0
O-10	3	0	3	0.0
Total	7,164	914	8,078	11.3

SOURCE: Surface Warfare community.
NOTE: All data are as of January 2001 and include Individuals Account.

Table 3.44

Retention Among Surface
Warfare Officers, by Gender

Fiscal	Retention at 9 Years of Service (%)	
Year	Overall	Female
1989	27	23.1
1990	24	9.8
1991	23	27.3
1992	29	14.8
1993	26	26.5

SOURCE: Navy Surface Warfare community.

groups in the Navy surface warfare community, at the nine-year point, both overall and women only. The Navy believes that tracking data at the nine-year point will identify individuals who are likely to stay to retirement in the absence of a vested retirement plan. Within this data set, the retention rates for women were dramatically different for some years, largely because there are relatively few women in the occupation, but were similar to those overall for other years.

The surface warfare community has evidence that female junior officers may separate early in their careers at rates nominally higher than those of their male peers; female SWOs stay to seven years of service at two-thirds the rate of their male peers. To date, the women who stay past the seven-year mark tend to retain in later years much like their male peers. However, it is not clear, as discussed earlier, whether the women currently entering the SWO community will retain at the same rates as those who qualified before the combat exclusion reversal.

Observations

Small numbers of women had careers in surface warfare while combatant ships were still closed to women. However, since the lifting of the combat exclusion, the number of female officer accessions in surface warfare has increased significantly.

When combatant ships were opened to women, almost all assignments in the surface warfare community opened to female officers; the few assignments that remain closed are unlikely to hamper opportunities for success among the female officers.

The women who entered the surface warfare community during the combat exclusion have shown high levels of commitment and resulting high levels of success, as measured by command opportunities. The women who entered after the combat exclusion was rescinded may well behave differently from the earlier cohorts. The data suggest that the retention rates for some of the younger women differ slightly from those of their male peers. However, current data indicate that the younger cohort of women is being offered prominent opportunities (such as department head assignments) at the same rate as their male peer group and that women who remain past seven years of service behave like their male peers thereafter.

In summary, gender integration of the surface warfare community is progressing well, and female officers who choose surface warfare have complete career opportunities. The increasing numbers of women in this occupation result in part from new opportunities for women and in part from remaining limits on what other warfare opportunities are available to women. The Navy will require more time to ascertain whether surface warfare retention rates will differ by gender because it is not clear whether women entering this occupation today will behave as did those who entered before.

Chapter Four

CONCLUSIONS, RECOMMENDATIONS, AND POLICY IMPLICATIONS

VALUE AND LIMITATIONS OF ANALYSIS

In the initial statistical analysis conducted for this research, we addressed gender representation in military occupations but did not attempt to determine the correct level of representation. Absent high-level guidance from Congress, policymakers, or the military services, it is unclear what the integration target should be. Lacking policy or legal guidance on integration targets, we chose to compare the level of representation to that of the appropriate service and note statistically significant differences in representation. Representation levels differ among occupations for multiple reasons. A primary factor is time elapsed; completely integrating an occupation does take a full career path cycle. There are also valid reasons, such as limited assignment opportunities, to limit the number of women in some occupations. Thus, we assert that this statistical "underrepresentation" or "overrepresentation" should be considered only as a benchmarking data point for comparison with future studies and in concert with qualitative evaluations or occupations, such as that conducted in the second half of our research.

The qualitative portion of this research investigated only a limited number of occupations; thus, the findings from this research may not be representative of other occupations recently opened to women. Nonetheless, the patterns from these occupations suggest issues that might also apply to other occupations. Additionally, lessons learned from these occupations suggest some policy changes or necessary research to determine whether these findings are indicative of similar situations in other occupations.

CONCLUSIONS

Table 4.1 summarizes the occupations described in Chapter Three. The columns briefly summarize the nature of the work involved; the current female representation, both by number and by percentage; whether the female representation is increasing; how the percentage of female accessions for the occupation compares to that for the service overall; and whether there are assignment restrictions and resultant career progression issues. The table is organized into three sections, each of which begins on a new page: career areas with little progress in gender integration, those with some progress, and those with more progress. The division into these categories is subjective.

The aviation occupations are among the group of occupations that still have relatively low percentages of women. Within this trio, however, the numbers of women among Army aviators and Air Force pilots seem to be increasing, while the Marine Corps has only a single female F/A-18 pilot. The numbers of women Marine Corps combat engineers have been increasing, but female accessions were zeroed out to reflect restricted assignment opportunities.

Four occupations had integrated to double-digit percentages. While the trend in three of the four is toward increasing representation, the numbers in the fourth, female Marine Corps Air Support Operators (7242), have remained fairly constant over the past few years (resulting in decreasing percentages of women). The trends that emerged from this analysis, some of which are apparent in the table, are discussed below.

It is worth noting, however, that the occupations with the most progress with respect to gender integration include one Army occupation, one Marine Corps occupation, and two Navy occupations. They include both officer and enlisted occupations, a range of environments, and both demanding physical labor and highly technical work. These differences underscore the extent to which gender analysis should consider occupations individually.

Female Representation

Half the occupations considered in this analysis show increasing female representation. The representation of women in one of the Army occupations, Bridge Crewmember, is higher than that of

Table 4.1
Summary of Occupations Examined

Occupation	Nature of Work	Female[a] No.	%	Occupational Class	% Female Increasing	Accessions Compared to Service Overall	Training Completion Rates Compared to Males	Assignment or Career Restrictions
Little Progress Toward Gender Integration								
Air Force F-16 Pilot (Officer)	Fighter aviation High tech.	21	1.30	Tactical Operations	?	N/A: Pilots	Comparable	None
USMC F/A-18 Pilot (Officer)	Fighter aviation High tech.	1	0.25	Tactical Operations	No	N/A: Pilots	N/A—numbers too small	One nonflying assignment closed No career impact
USMC Combat Engineer (1371) (Enlisted)	Heavy, dirty Field conditions	34	1.30	Infantry, Gun Crews, and Seamanship	No	Lower	Comparable or better	Yes—46% closed Career impact

Table 4.1—Continued

Occupation	Nature of Work	Female[a] No.	%	Occupational Class	% Female Increasing	Accessions Compared to Service Overall	Training Completion Rates Compared to Males	Assignment or Career Restrictions
Some Progress Toward Gender Integration								
Army AH-64 Apache Aviator (152F/H) (Warrant Officer)	Helicopter aviation High tech.	14	1.36	Tactical Operations	Yes	N/A: Pilots	Comparable	None
Army Field Artillery Surveyor (82C) (Enlisted)	Dirty Field conditions	52	7.00	Other Technical and Allied Specialist	No	Lower	Comparable	Yes—70% closed Career impact, job being phased out
Navy Gunner's Mate (Enlisted)	Diverse condition Extensive sea duty	183	4.35	Infantry, Gun Crews, and Seamanship	Yes, slowly	Lower	Comparable	Yes, smaller ships No career impact

Table 4.1—Continued

Occupation	Nature of Work	Female[a] No.	Female[a] %	Occupational Class	% Female Increasing	Accessions Compared to Service Overall	Training Completion Rates Compared to Males	Assignment or Career Restrictions
Most Progress Toward Gender Integration								
Army Bridge Crewmember (12C) (Enlisted)	Heavy, dirty Field conditions	148	16.53	Infantry, Gun Crews, and Seamanship	Yes	Higher	Lower	None
USMC Air Support (7242) (Enlisted)	Field conditions	27	11.00	Communications and Intelligence Specialists	No	Comparable	Comparable	None currently applied
Navy Sonar Technician-Surface (Enlisted)	High tech Extensive sea duty	389	10.13	Electronic Equipment Repairers	Yes	Comparable	Slightly lower	Yes, smaller ships No career impact
Navy Surface Warfare Officer (Officer)	Extensive sea duty	914	1.30	Tactical Operations	Yes	Higher	Comparable	Very few, very small ships No career impact

aData as of 2001.

women in the Army overall and is still increasing. The Army aviation occupation is relatively static. The Army Artillery Surveyor occupation currently includes 7 percent women but should cease to accept any more, given the lack of a future for them. The numbers of women in the Air Force occupation studied (F-16 pilots) and in all the Navy occupations are increasing. It is not clear from this analysis why Marine Corps F/A-18 pilots have not integrated at a rate similar to that of Air Force F-16 pilots. Of the other Marine Corps occupations, female representation among Air Support Operators holds steady at a rate higher than that among Marine Corps enlisted personnel overall. Representation among Marine Corps Combat Engineers is considerably lower, and the Marine Corps plans to keep it at approximately this level.

In three of the four occupations that indicate significant progress in gender integration, representation is increasing. In three of the four occupations that show little progress, gender representation is not increasing. The in-between category is split evenly. Having noted that, however, it is difficult to assign an analytical importance for gender representation to this measure without delving into the particulars of each occupation. If an occupation has reached an ideal level of gender representation, the percentage of women in that occupation should remain relatively static. However, this analysis highlights that the "ideal" level of female representation is not clear. For example, Table 4.1 displays the Marine Corps Combat Engineer occupation among the occupations that show little progress. This placement is a judgment call, given that the Marine Corps could claim that integration of this occupation is complete. On the other hand, female representation among Navy SWOs is increasing. Those who want the SWO community to be fully integrated might consider this a positive trend, while others might view it simply as a reflection of the limited options for female officers in the rest of the unrestricted line (which also includes submarine and aviation officers).

Nature of the Work

The nature of the work, whether it is conducted in field conditions or involves heavy or dirty work, does not drive the number of women who are attracted to an occupation. Being an Army Bridge Crewmember or a Marine Corps Air Support Operations Operator involves living in austere field conditions. Bridge Crewmember is also classified as having very heavy physical requirements. Nonetheless, the populations of both occupations have greater percentages of female personnel than do their services overall. Other occupations that were analyzed, such as Navy Gunner's Mates and Marine Corps Combat Engineers, are also dirty or physically demanding but have much lower levels of female representation. The Navy Sonar Technician occupation, which is described as cleaner and more highly technical, has lower female representation than does the Navy enlisted population as a whole, but the representation is increasing.

Among the aviation occupations considered—Air Force F-16 pilots, Marine Corps F/A-18 pilots, and Army Apache aviators—none of the populations includes large numbers or percentages of female pilots. Nonetheless, Army Apache aviators includes 1.36-percent women, which is more than either of the other occupations. While the fixed-wing aviation occupations may be perceived to be less welcoming to women, our study was unable to support that assertion. Instead, recent findings show that women are declining opportunities to fly jet aircraft. It is not evident, however, why the Air Force has had slightly greater success in increasing the number of female F-16 pilots than the Marine Corps has had with F/A-18 pilots.

Accession and Training

The occupations vary in whether the female portion of their accessions was higher than, comparable to, or lower than that of the respective service, and this measurement appears key to the overall level of representation in the career. The occupation with the highest accession rates among those we studied (Army Bridge Crewmembers) shows an increasing number of women. Two of the three occupations that have lower accession rates (Army Artillery Surveyor, Marine Corps Combat Engineer, and Navy Gunner's Mates) than their services did not evidence increasing representation within the career, although the percentage of Gunner's Mates who are women is slowly increasing.

The female representation among accessions for all four of the more-integrated occupations was comparable to or greater than that for the respective services. This is not surprising; if the percentage of women brought into an occupation exceeds the percentage of women in the service, the relative percentage of women will always increase. However, targets for female accessions are dictated by service models that consider the ideal numbers of women in any occupation, given their assignment opportunities. These models limit the overall number of women in occupations, so positive performance and retention of women in these occupations can actually reduce the future accession targets for women (because large numbers are staying). Concurrent RAND Arroyo Center analysis of Army models has suggested that some of the model inputs and calculations may need to be revisited and that the models may thus be more restrictive about female accessions than policy would suggest.

The ideal number of female Marines in any given occupation is an especially difficult issue, and one that the Marine Corps is currently reassessing. The service's models appear to be especially limiting in the case of the Marine Corps Combat Engineer, which is being held at approximately 1.3 percent female, even though over half of the assignment opportunities are open to women. The issue of gender as part of force planning modeling is extremely complex and warrants further examination, such as that conducted for the Army. It does not appear to be in the interest of either the Marine Corps or the individual service member to fill an occupation with more women than can have a viable career, given limited assignment opportunities. However, the decision processes, assumptions, and model calculations that produce accession targets by gender are not immediately evident or easily evaluated, making it difficult to verify that 1.3 percent is the ideal level.

In general, training rates indicated that women could perform on a par with their male colleagues in training. Training graduation rates were often difficult to analyze, given small numbers, but it appeared that women were, over time, performing either as well as their male peers or only slightly lower. In the case of Army Bridge Crewmembers, the male trainees graduated at higher rates than did the female trainees, but the women still graduated at rates above 80 percent. Female Sonar Technicians also tended to graduate from skill training at rates slightly lower than those of their male peers, but nearing 80 percent. This research found nothing to suggest that female trainees will have any problem performing well in nontraditional skill training.

An important consideration in the analysis of accession and training data is whether women are hindered from pursuing military occupations. The accession process for each occupation examined differs somewhat. To the degree that the services are "hindering" the progress of integration, this research found barriers or resistance embodied only in accession restrictions or assignment (and sometimes resultant advancement) opportunities. For many military occupations, some level of restriction on accessions and assignments is appropriate. However, as stated previously, the logic for determining these levels is not always apparent, and the determinations seem likely to be taking place at relatively low policy levels.

Another accession and training consideration relates to ASVAB scoring. GAO findings suggest that women score less well on certain components of the ASVAB because they lack exposure to certain subjects. Additionally, DMDC research has quantified the effects of prior exposure on four of the ASVAB tests. This research found that exposure to content accounted for a relatively large portion of differences in test scores between males and females. The research also found that while male and female subjects' Armed Forces Qualification Test scores differed by less than one-tenth of a standard deviation, they differed by more than one-third of a standard deviation on GS and by more than a full standard deviation on Auto and Shop Information (AS) (American Institute for Research, 1997).

While our research did not investigate the ASVAB scores of female recruits in general, we did find that the services did not generally have problems recruiting sufficient numbers of female recruits to these nontraditional occupations to satisfy service recruiting targets and that sufficient numbers of women passed their skill training. Thus, scoring less well than men on certain components of the ASVAB does not currently limit the integration of women into the selected occupations. Nonetheless, it appears likely that the ASVAB prerequisites could limit female participation in some occupations not included among our case studies or that the prerequisites could affect female participation in these occupations if the female accession targets were increased.

Occupation Assignment Patterns

This research explored formal assignment opportunities for female service members in the selected occupations, as well as the effects of gender-limited assignments on male service members. When there are assignment constraints, gender integration in the occupation is often considered problematic. Two of the occupations considered have severe assignment constraints. The Marine Corps has zeroed out the female accession targets to limit the number of women among Combat Engineers, and the Army is phasing out Artillery Surveyor by merging it with occupations that are closed to women. Neither occupation offers opportunities for advancement and success to female service members. The civilian-transferable skills Combat Engineer provides may compensate for the limited opportunities individuals have while in uniform. Regardless, female recruits should be counseled about the limited number of opportunities available to them if they choose this occupation.

Several of the occupations discussed have much-less-limiting assignment constraints. As described in Chapter Two, female enlisted Navy personnel cannot serve on frigates or smaller surface ships or on ships that are scheduled for integration but that are not yet available to female enlisted personnel. Female officers can serve on almost all surface ships except patrol craft. The smaller ships are not considered necessarily career enhancing for Navy personnel, but then there is also no evidence that male careers are unduly hampered by filling these assignments.

The perceived differences between assignments that are open or closed to women within a career might have two different kinds of effects. If women are precluded from career-enhancing assignments or jobs perceived as being key to occupational development (such as assignments in tactical level units), women are unlikely to be evaluated as highly and are thus unlikely to experience the same levels of career success. If women are precluded from filling assignments that are considered to be less attractive or even detrimental to careers, women might find themselves resented by their male peers. In these instances, a cultural resistance to gender integration can develop. Such cultural resistance is increasingly likely as larger numbers of women populate such occupations, enhancing the perception that men are taking "more than their fair share" of less-appealing assignments.

Predicting Future Levels of Gender Integration

Several issues hamper the ability to predict future levels of gender integration. First, when individuals do not enter directly into an occupation, such as when there is a lengthy training and selection process (as for aviation occupations), it is difficult to analyze and assess the factors that influence the process of integration.

Second, while the relationships among accession, retention, and representation should be relatively clear in larger populations, small numbers (especially in retention figures) complicate any prediction. Service commitments, such as those for flight training, also complicate and obscure retention conclusions. In these instances, the communities will suffer the problems of extrapolating from small numbers several years hence, and it will be even longer before larger numbers of women progress through their obligated service and contribute to a more-comprehensive understanding of whether women will retain in patterns similar to those of their male peers.

Third, most of the women in these newly opened occupations can still be considered "pioneers." Given any cultural resistance or other perceived difficulties that pioneers in a field may experience, they may either leave at higher rates or exhibit greater determination and resultant success than will later women who are not part of the pioneer phase. Most of the occupations described in this report might still be considered within the pioneer phase, although currently entering SWOs are likely postpioneer. Occupations in which there has been little or slow progress in gender integration, such as aviation, will take considerably longer to emerge from the pioneer phase. The duration of the pioneer phase makes assessment of progress, as well as the eventual steady state of behavioral patterns and resultant levels of integration, difficult to predict and plan for.

RECOMMENDATIONS AND POLICY IMPLICATIONS

Recognize that female representation needs to be understood by occupation.

Do not assume that female service members will lack interest in jobs with seemingly less-appealing work environments.

Counsel incoming personnel about the career opportunities available to them in various occupations. If no advancement opportunities are available within a given occupation, the incoming recruit should be informed. Lack of opportunities for promotion may dissuade a new recruit from selecting that occupation. However, if the skills to be gained translate well to civilian occupations (as is the case, for example for Marine Corps Combat Engineers), limited opportunities within the military occupation may not deter accessions. While this is more likely to be an issue for women entering occupations with limited assignment opportunities for women (and thus limited advancement opportunities), both male and female recruits should fully understand the career opportunities available to them.

When an occupation is to be closed to women or is being merged into an occupation that is closed to women, cease accepting women into the occupation and plan opportunities to be made available to women currently in that occupation.

Ensure that publicly available information, such as that on official recruiting Web sites, provides accurate information about opportunities available to women.

Recognize that individual and systemic behavior in newly integrated occupations will be influenced by the pioneer effect for an undefined amount of time and, thus, that assertions about the success of integration, the ability of female personnel to perform on a par with their male colleagues, or retention behavior may be premature.

Promote analysis of trends in accession, training, assignment, and retention data by gender. "Gender-blind" data records serve little purpose other than to simplify the daily activities of those who maintain the records. Such records obscure both negative and positive trends. As a result, the services recognize neither when they need to address problems nor when they can applaud successful integration and capitalize on positive trends.

Conduct further research into the role of individual experiences and decisionmaking processes in occupation selection, assignment selection, and retention.

Conduct further research to understand the role of individual decisionmaking in aircraft selection. Such research should illuminate the reasons quality flight students, both male and female, are neglecting to fly jet aircraft.

Verify and validate the service models that limit female accessions as a result of assignments closed to women.

BIBLIOGRAPHY

American Institute for Research, *Item Evaluation for the Armed Services Vocational Aptitude Battery (ASVAB) Science and Technical Test Specifications: Conduct Exposure to Content Analysis,* Arlington, Va.: Defense Manpower Data Center, December 1997.

Army—See U.S. Army.

Aspin, Les, Policy on Assignment of Women in the Armed Forces, memorandum from the Secretary of Defense, Washington, D.C., April 28, 1993.

_____, Direct Ground Combat Definition and Assignment Rule, memorandum from the Secretary of Defense, Washington, D.C., January 13, 1994.

Beckett, Megan, and Sandy Chien, *The Status of Gender Integration in the Military: Supporting Appendices,* Santa Monica, Calif.: RAND, MR-1381-OSD, 2002.

GAO—See U.S. General Accounting Office.

Harrell, Margaret C., and Laura L. Miller, *New Opportunities for Military Women: Effects on Readiness, Cohesion, and Morale,* Santa Monica, Calif.: RAND, MR-896-OSD, 1997.

Heines, Vivienne, "For Skilled Aviators, the Sky's No Limit," *Navy Times,* December 11, 2000a, pp. 13–14.

Heines, Vivienne, "Wave Off," *Navy Times,* December 11, 2000b, pp. 12–14.

Holm, Jeanne, *Women in the Military: An Unfinished Revolution,* Navato, California: Presidio Press, 1982.

House—See U.S. House of Representatives.

U.S. Army, "Alternate Flight Aptitude Selection Test (AFAST) Information Pamphlet, Washington, D.C., Headquarters, Department of the Army, Pamphlet 611-256-2," March 1, 1987.

U.S. Army, Alternate Flight Aptitude Selection Test (AFAST) Information, February 4, 1999a.   Online at http://www-rucker.army.mil/AP/AP/recruit/AFAST.htm (as of April 11, 2002).

_____, "Military Occupational Classification and Structure," Washington, D.C., Headquarters, Department of the Army, Pamphlet 611-21, March 31, 1999b.

_____, Field Artillery Surveyor job description, June 26, 2000.   Online at http://media.goarmy.com/activedata/mosdesc.asp?MOS=82C (as of April 11, 2002).

_____, Military Occupational Specialty pages, March 14, 2002.   Online at http://www.goarmy.com/jobs/ as of April 11, 2002.

U.S. Department of Labor, Employment and Training Administration, *Dictionary of Occupational Titles,* 4th ed., Washington, D.C., 1991.

U.S. General Accounting Office, *Gender Issues: Information to Assess Service Members' Perceptions of Gender Inequities Is Incomplete,* NSIAD-99-27, November 1998.

_____, *Gender Issues: Trends in Occupational Distribution of Military Women,* NSIAD-99-212, September 1999.

U.S. House of Representatives, Legislative History, House Report No. 103-200 Section 542-Gender Neutral Occupational Performance Standards, undated.

_____, Committee on National Security, *National Defense Authorization Act for Fiscal Year 1997: Conference Report to Accompany H.R. 3230, Subtitle B—Force Structure,* 104th Congress, 2nd Session, 1996, House Report 104-724. Washington, D.C.: U.S. Government Printing Office, 1996.

_____, National Defense Authorization Act for Fiscal Year 1997, Report of the Committee on National Security, House of Representatives on H. R. 3230 Together with Additional, Supplemental, and Dissenting Views (Including Cost Estimate of the Congressional Budget Office), Washington, D.C.: U.S. Government Printing Office, 1996.

USMC—See U.S. Marine Corps.

U.S. Marine Corps, *MOS Manual*, MCO P1200.7V, undated z.

_____, recruiting and training materials, undated b.

_____, Memorandum, Deputy Commandant for Aviation, 1300 AVN, May 5, 2000.

U.S. Navy, "Gunner's Mate (GM) Rating Card," February 1999a.

_____, "Sonar Technician, Surface (STG) Rating Card," February 1999b.

_____, "Sonar Technician, Surface (STG-AEF) Rating Card," February 1999c.